★

ICONS

# 70ˢ FASHION

## VINTAGE FASHION AND BEAUTY ADS

Ed. Jim Heimann

Introduction by Laura Schooling

**TASCHEN**

HONG KONG  KÖLN  LONDON  LOS ANGELES  MADRID  PARIS  TOKYO

Front cover: *Smitty Cologne, 1972*
Back cover: *Jesus Jeans, 1976*
Endpapers: *After Six, 1972*
Facing title page: *Coats & Clark, 1972*
Inside back page: *Halston, 1977*

All images are from the Jim Heimann collection unless otherwise noted.
Any omissions for copy or credit are unintentional, and appropriate credit will
be given in future editions if such copyright holders contact the publisher.

**Dates in captions refer to the year of the advertisement's publication and not
necessarily the year in which the product was manufactured.**

To stay informed about upcoming TASCHEN titles, please request our magazine
at www.taschen.com/magazine or write to TASCHEN, Hohenzollernring 53,
D-50672 Cologne, Germany, contact@taschen.com, Fax: +49-221-254919.
We will be happy to send you a free copy of our magazine, which is filled with
information about all of our books.

© 2006 TASCHEN GmbH
Hohenzollernring 53, D-50672 Köln
**www.taschen.com**

Editor: Jim Heimann, Los Angeles
Design and editorial coordination: Stephen Schmidt / Duuplex, San Mateo
Design assistant: Sophia Valko, Moss Beach
Production: Morgan Slade, Los Angeles
Project management: Florian Kobler & Barbara Huttrop, Cologne
English-language editors: Kate Soto & Anna Skinner, Los Angeles
German translation: Henriette Zeltner, Munich
French translation: Alice Pétillot, Charenton-le-Pont
Collaboration: Daphne Rozenblatt, Los Angeles

Printed in Italy
ISBN 978-8228-4937-8

# Fashion on the Fringes

## by Laura Schooling

By the beginning of the seventies, the peace movement of the previous decade's final years had become rife with pessimism. When embattled soldiers finally returned home from Vietnam in 1973, a majority of Americans were disillusioned and distrustful of their government. Positive social change was heavily afoot, however, thanks to the civil rights and women's movements gaining speed. As many people fought to regain a sense of normalcy amid the political and cultural turmoil, others were swept up in the momentum of change and demanded revolution at any cost. Fashion was equally duplicitous, with the mainstream playing it straight and subtle and the few on the fringes consumed with fantasy and revolution.

The fledgling *Rolling Stone* magazine provided national visibility for the music heroes of the day, and their wardrobes, as fashion became as instrumental to a musician's career as the music itself. The frenzy of sixties' psychedelia had crested and crashed before the end of 1970 as two larger-than-life prodigies fatally succumbed to the scene's inherent excess. Jimi Hendrix and Janis Joplin, who overdosed within months of each other, were superlatives of the psychedelic look, with unkempt hair, piles of beads, long tasseled vests, velvet jackets, billowing sleeves, and fabrics in an array of colors and textures. More subtly, Bob Dylan's suede jackets and wide-brimmed hats and Joni Mitchell's straight center-parted hair and calf-skimming skirts reflected the folk aesthetic. The Beatles disbanded in 1970 and John Lennon became inseparable from Yoko Ono, with the two of them wearing all-white robes or nothing at all. Look-alike couples were a new trend, and haircuts melded into middle-of-the-road unisex lengths, as witnessed by Paul and Linda McCartney's band (and hairstyles), Wings. But nobody's vision of androgyny could match David Bowie, who in 1972 introduced a new persona, Ziggy Stardust. His gender-neutral alter ego, complete with exaggerated makeup and glittering bodysuits, created a stage spectacle that prepped the mainstream for an increasingly open gay movement.

Bowie posed with Twiggy on the cover of his 1973 album *Pin Ups*, an event she recalls as one of the most thrilling of her career. The sixties' modeling icon officially retired as a cover girl at the start of the seventies, making room for a new crop of fresh faces: Margaux Hemingway, Lauren Hutton, and Beverly Johnson—the first black model to appear on the cover of *Vogue*. The look was all-American and accessible, with diverse representations of women: from the wide-eyed ingénue to the business executive. Glitz and glamour could be found at rock shows, but in magazines, models were buttoned-up and toned-down.

The Safari jacket that Yves Saint Laurent introduced in 1968 was still popular and widely copied by 1973, but few other mainstays of the previous decade's fashion translated to the seventies. The once ubiquitous miniskirt was replaced by hot pants, which revealed as much leg as its skirt counterpart while providing the comfort to dance, roller-skate, or even fight crime, as TV's Wonder Woman ably demonstrated from 1976 to 1979. Found in velvet, denim, metallic—just about

Top: *Jantzen, 1976*    Bottom: *Sunkist, 1973*

any fabric—they were often paired with square-heeled boots or platform clogs to further elongate the legs. Skirt hemlines, however, plummeted below the knee (midi) and even to the floor (maxi). Bell-bottoms and flares transitioned from the hippie movement to urban funk and disco wear. From denim to jumpsuits, the fit was as tight as possible at the hips down to a full swing around the ankles.

As French and Italian couturiers continued a dominant reign, American designers were also coming into their own. Halston was celebrated for his beautiful, flowing, seamless dresses in the early part of the decade. And later, as disco caught on, he was the go-to designer for socialites like Bianca Jagger and Jerry Hall. Calvin Klein packaged his brand as a lifestyle. Aided by controversial photographer Helmut Newton, he put as much emphasis on the body as the clothes. Sexuality was sold alongside his streamlined designs and neutral colors. Ralph Lauren elaborated on his newly successful menswear line—distinguished by its flamboyant ties—by creating a version for women. As the women's movement gained momentum, a defining wardrobe was needed to accompany newly available positions of power. Trouser-wearing icons such as Katharine Hepburn were often cited as inspiration, and designers sought to make womenswear that was beautifully suited for an independent woman. Ralph Lauren was responsible for popularizing menswear for women in 1977, as the designer of Diane Keaton's famous masculine-influenced wardrobe in *Annie Hall*. But Lauren and Klein probably made the greatest impact with their contribution to denim, introducing one of the fashion world's most profitable and lasting endeavors—designer jeans.

Denim covered everything from purses to pillows and was worn by everyone from cowboys to college girls. Casual comfort reached new heights with the popularity of corduroy, which transformed men's fashion. Often manufactured in brown, tan, and other autumnal colors, corduroy was used to create everything from everyday slacks to three-piece suits. The look was best brought to life in 1977 by the character of Jack Tripper on the TV series *Three's Company*; conversely, the more ornate leisure suit and cravat was perversely worn by the show's Mr. Furley.

Between 1970 and 1977, popular styles were modeled for an American audience by the beloved working girl of the eponymous hit TV show, Mary Tyler Moore. Her look evolved with the decade, starting with perfectly flipped hair and skirt suits and progressing to include sheepskin coats, head scarves, tunic suits, and flattering wrap dresses by Diane Von Furstenberg. But nobody changed the working wardrobe like Giorgio Armani, whose legend was born with his androgynous suits for women and understated cuts for men. He approached fashion with the mind-set of an artisan tailor and dominated the fads of fashion with his clean, tailored, yet casual style.

The concept of "personal style" was spawned by the antifashion movement of the early seventies, which married "retro" thrift store finds from previous decades, cast-off military garb, and less expensive store-bought garments. Toward the end of the decade the fashion forward were better known for their individuality than for having the latest "it" item. Everyone wore jeans and T-shirts and could look to a multitude of emerging designers with varying inspirations for new fashion freedom. Geoffrey Beene applauded clean lines and discouraged overaccessorizing; Laura Ashley popu-

Bottom: *Pierre Cardin, 1971*    Top: *Eminence Paris, 1977*

larized Victorian-era simplicity; and Agnes B. designed understated French staples. Regardless of influence, individualism was the greatest fashion of all.

When disco came along, with punk rock fast on its heels, fashion ambiguity came to an end. In 1974 the Watergate scandal further withered America's opinion of the White House, and in 1975 Margaret Thatcher became the U. K.'s first female Prime Minister. Both nations were in deep recessions, with unemployment and discontent welling up, especially in the working class. The U. S. aimed to overwhelm the doldrums with the shiny excess of disco. *Saturday Night Fever* hit the theaters in 1977, and John Travolta pointed and thrusted his way across the lit-up dance floor in his Angel Flight suit to the delight of women decked-out in Lycra cat suits and polyester halter dresses. America clamored for clothing that would sparkle under a disco ball, and New York's Studio 54 opened that same year, becoming the epicenter of seventies' decadence, best demonstrated by Bianca Jagger's entrance into the club on a white horse led by a naked, body-painted man. Subtlety was not an issue, as most subscribed to the ideal of the bigger the better. Neckties the size of dish towels, platform heels, shoulder-grazing earrings, feathered hair, bold belt buckles, and whatever else could be emphasized—from clothing to the physical attributes that lay underneath—were celebrated for their size.

On the other side of the Atlantic, Johnnie Rotten sang about "no future" as he and the Sex Pistols destroyed any established idea of fashion and conformity by purposefully ripping their clothing—and reattaching it with safety pins—spiking their hair, and adorning their dark denim and leather clothes with symbols of anarchy. To their chagrin, their fans and millions of disenfranchised youth would soon co-opt those attempts at antifashion and turn them into the uniform of the antiestablishment. Vivienne Westwood put the stamp on punk fashion when she created an image of the Queen of England with a pin through her nose.

Punk proliferated across the U. K. and U. S. as motorcycle jacket-wearing bands like the Clash and the Ramones redirected youth angst into three-chord songs. New York's CBGB club introduced bands like Television and the Talking Heads, who garnered attention with off-kilter vocals and ill-fitting suits, while Blondie's Deborah Harry captivated audiences with sultry vocals and stiletto boots. Whether one emulated the New York punk scene or tripped out to the Grateful Dead, fashion, more than ever, offered people the freedom to follow their own beat.

Above: *Duke, 1970*

# Fransen am Rande

## von Laura Schooling

Anfang der 1970er-Jahre wurde die Friedensbewegung zunehmend von Pessimismus geprägt. Als die Soldaten 1973 endlich aus Vietnam heimkehrten, hatte die Mehrheit der Amerikaner das Vertrauen in ihre Regierung verloren. Doch dank der sich immer stärker durchsetzenden Bürgerrechts- und Frauenbewegung kam es auch zu positiven gesellschaftlichen Veränderungen. Während viele Menschen in diesen politischen und kulturellen Wirren um eine gewisse Normalität rangen, wurden andere von dem Schwung der Veränderung mitgerissen und forderten Revolution um jeden Preis. Die Einstellung zur Mode war ebenso gespalten, die Mehrheit kleidete sich mal schlicht, mal raffiniert, während die wenigen Randgruppen in Fantasie und Revolution schwelgten.

Die neu gegründete Zeitschrift *Rolling Stone* machte die aktuellen Musikidole und ihre Kleidung landesweit bekannt, denn schon damals war die Mode für die Karriere eines Musikers ebenso entscheidend wie die Musik selbst. Die psychedelischen Auswüchse der Sixties erreichten noch im Jahr 1970 einen vorläufigen Höhe- und Endpunkt, als zwei überlebensgroße Talente den szeneüblichen Exzessen zum Opfer fielen. Jimi Hendrix und Janis Joplin, die sich innerhalb weniger Monaten eine Überdosis verpassten, waren Ikonen des psychedelischen Looks gewesen. Sie trugen ungekämmte Haare, haufenweise Perlen, lange Fransenwesten, Samtjacken, bauschige Ärmel und Stoffe in allen nur erdenklichen Farben und Strukturen. Dagegen waren die Wildlederjacken und breitkrempigen Hüte von Bob Dylan sowie die glatten Haare mit Mittelscheitel und wadenlangen Röcke von Joni Mitchell deutlich unauffälliger, die sich eher an einer folkloristischen Ästhetik anlehnten. 1970 trennten sich die Beatles, während John Lennon und Yoko Ono fortan unzertrennlich waren und sich entweder in weißen Wallekleidern oder ganz nackt präsentierten. Der Partnerlook lag im Trend, und die Frisuren verschmolzen zu einer Einheitslänge für beide Geschlechter, was man an den Wings, der Band von Paul und Linda McCartney hervorragend beobachten kann. Eine unübertroffene Vision von Androgynität gelang jedoch David Bowie mit seiner Figur Ziggy Stardust. Sein geschlechtsneutrales Alter Ego, mit übertrieben viel Make-up und glitzernden Bodys, sorgte für ein Bühnenspektakel, das die breite Öffentlichkeit auf die zunehmend selbstbewusstere Homosexuellenbewegung vorbereitete.

Bowie posierte 1973 mit Twiggy auf dem Cover seines Albums *Pin Ups*, was diese rückblickend als einen der aufregendsten Momente ihrer Karriere empfand. Die Model-Ikone der Sechziger zog sich zu Beginn der 1970er-Jahre offiziell als Covergirl zurück und machte für eine neue Generation frischer Gesichter Platz: Margaux Hemingway, Lauren Hutton und Beverly Johnson – das erste schwarze Model auf der Titelseite der *Vogue*. Ihr Look war ebenso amerikanisch wie tragbar und spiegelte verschiedene Frauentypen wider: von der naiven Unschuld mit den großen Augen bis hin zur Managerin. Glitzer und Glamour konnte man bei Bühnenshows bewundern, doch in den Zeitschriften wirkten die Models zugeknöpft und zurückgenommen.

Die 1968 von Yves Saint Laurent eingeführte Safarijacke war auch 1973 noch gefragt und wurde oft kopiert. Doch abgesehen davon überlebten in den Siebzigern nur wenige Modeklassiker des vorangegangenen Jahrzehnts. Den einst allgegenwärtigen Minirock ersetzten die Hotpants, die genau so viel Bein zeigten, aber die Möglichkeit boten, darin zu tanzen, Rollschuh zu fahren, ja sogar Verbrecher zu bekämpfen, wie Wonder Woman es von 1976 bis 1979 im Fernsehen demonstrierte. Oft trug man sie zu Stiefeln mit Blockabsatz oder Clogs mit Plateausohlen, um die Beine optisch zu verlängern. Die Rocksäume fielen bis unters Knie (Midi) oder sogar bis zum Boden (Maxi). Schlaghosen wurden aus der Hippie-Bewegung in die urbane Funk- und Discomode gerettet.

Obwohl die französischen und italienischen Couturiers den Ton angaben, konnten sich die amerikanischen Designer ebenfalls behaupten. Halston wurde zu Beginn dieses Jahrzehnts für seine wunderschönen fließenden und nahtlosen Kleider gefeiert. Als sich der Discotrend immer stärker durchsetzte, war er der Promi-Designer schlechthin für Frauen wie Bianca Jagger und Jerry Hall. Calvin Klein machte aus seiner Marke gleich einen ganzen Lifestyle. Mit Hilfe des damals umstrittenen Fotografen Helmut Newton schenkte er dem Körper ebensoviel Augenmerk wie der Kleidung.

Sexualität wurde mit seinen stromlinienförmigen Entwürfen und neutralen Farben gleich mitverkauft. Ralph Lauren erweiterte seine erst seit kurzem erfolgreiche Herrenlinie – die vor allem durch ihre extravaganten Krawatten auffiel – und ergänzte sie um eine Kollektion für Damen. Da die Frauenbewegung zunehmend an Bedeutung gewann, bedurfte es einer entsprechenden Garderobe für jene Frauen, die neuerdings einflussreiche Positionen bekleideten. Hosen tragende Vorbilder wie Katharine Hepburn dienten als vielzitierte Quellen der Inspiration, und die Designer versuchten eine Damenmode zu kreieren, die einer unabhängigen wie Frau auf den Leib geschneidert war. Ralph Lauren machte 1977 Herrenmode für Frauen tragbar, als er Diane Keatons berühmte maskulin geprägte Garderobe für *Annie Hall* entwarf. Den größten Einfluss nahmen Lauren und Klein jedoch mit ihren Beiträgen zum Thema Denim, als sie eine der profitabelsten und dauerhaftesten Errungenschaften in die Modewelt einführten – Designerjeans.

Denim war plötzlich überall, ob als Material für Portemonnaies oder Kissen, und wurde vom Cowboy bis zur Collegestudentin von jedermann getragen. Lässiger Komfort erreichte mit der Verbreitung von Cordstoffen, die wiederum die Herrenmode veränderten, einen neuen Höhepunkt. Meist wurde das Material in Braun, Ocker und anderen Herbsttönen verarbeitet und diente als Basis für alles mögliche, von Alltagshosen bis hin zu dreiteiligen Anzügen. Am besten wurde der Look 1977 durch die Rolle von Jack Tripper in der TV-Serie *Herzbube mit zwei Damen* verkörpert; die etwas chicere Variante mit Freizeitanzug und Krawatte trug in der Serie ausgerechnet Mr. Furley.

Zwischen 1970 und 1977 wurden dem amerikanischen Publikum die aktuellen Outfits von Mary Tyler Moore in der gleichnamigen TV-Erfolgsserie nahegebracht. Ihr Look wandelte sich im Laufe des Jahrzehnts von perfekt ondulierter Frisur und Kostümen bis hin zu Schaffellmänteln, um den Kopf geschlungenen Schals, Tuniken und schmeichelnden Wickelkleidern von Diane von Fürstenberg. Doch niemand hat die Mode der Berufstätigen derart beeinflusst wie Giorgio Armani, dessen Ruhm sich auf androgyne Hosenanzüge für Frauen und Understatement ausdrückende Schnitte für Herren gründete. Er begegnete der Mode mit dem Selbstverständnis eines Kunsthandwerkers und setzte diversen Modetorheiten seinen klaren, figurbetonten aber zugleich lässigen Stil entgegen.

Above: *Nadine, 1975*

Die Anti-Mode-Bewegung der frühen 1970er-Jahre brachte die Idee vom »individuellen Stil« hervor; diese kombinierte Retro-Fundstücke früherer Jahrzehnte aus Secondhand-Läden, abgelegte Uniformteile und preiswerte Kleidung von der Stange. Gegen Ende dieses Jahrzehnts waren modische Vorreiter eher für ihren Individualismus berühmt als dafür, die neuesten »Must-Haves« zu besitzen. Alle trugen Jeans und T-Shirt und konnten sich an einer Vielzahl aufstrebender Designer orientieren, was ihnen zu einer bislang ungekannten modischen Freiheit verhalf. Geoffrey Beene bevorzugte klare Schnitte und war gegen zu viele Accessoires; Laura Ashley machte die Schlichtheit des viktorianischen Zeitalters populär; und Agnes B. entwarf französische Massenartikel, die auf Understatement setzten. Unabhängig davon war Individualismus der vorherrschende Modetrend.

Als die Discowelle, rasch gefolgt vom Punk, aufkam, hatte es mit der modischen Vielfalt ein Ende. 1974 setzte der Watergate-Skandal dem Ansehen des Weißen Hauses noch weiter zu; 1975 wurde Margaret Thatcher die erste Frau im Amt des britischen Premierministers. Beide Länder steckten tief in der Rezession; Arbeitslosigkeit und Unzufriedenheit herrschten vor allem in der Arbeiterklasse. Amerika versuchte der allgemeinen Niedergeschlagenheit mit glitzernden Disco-Exzessen Herr zu werden. 1977 kam *Saturday Night Fever* in die Kinos, und John Travolta fuchtelte und wirbelte in seinem Angel-Flight-Kostüm über die illuminierte Tanzfläche, zur Freude der mit Catsuits aus Lycra und Miederkleidern aus Polyester angetanen Frauen. Amerika schrie nach Kleidung, die unter Discokugeln glitzerte. Im selben Jahr eröffnete das Studio 54 in New York und wurde sofort zum Mittelpunkt der Dekadenz der Siebzigerjahre, die niemand besser verkörperte als Bianca Jagger, als sie auf einem weißen Pferd in den Club einritt. Understatement war nicht gefragt, stattdessen herrschte die Überzeugung »je größer, desto besser«: Krawatten so groß wie Geschirrtücher, Plateauabsätze, Ohrringe bis zu den Schultern, auftoupierte Frisuren, monumentale Gürtelschnallen und alles, was sich irgendwie betonen ließ – von Kleidungsstücken bis hin zu den körperlichen Attributen darunter – wurden um seiner Größe willen gefeiert.

Auf der anderen Seite des Atlantik sang Johnnie Rotten von »no future«, während er und die Sex Pistols alle überkommenen Vorstellungen von Mode und Konformität zerstörten, indem sie ihre Kleidung absichtlich zerfetzten und mit Sicherheitsnadeln wieder zusammensteckten, Stachelfrisuren trugen und ihre dunklen Jeans- und Lederklamotten mit anarchistischen Symbolen versahen. Zu ihrem Missfallen entschieden sich ihre Fans und Millionen unterprivilegierter Jugendlicher bald ebenfalls für diese Form der Anti-Mode und verwandelten sie so in die Uniform des Anti-Establishments. Vivienne Westwood drückte der Punkmode ihren Stempel auf, als sie ein Bild der englischen Königin mit einer Sicherheitsnadel in der Nase kreierte.

Punk fand in Großbritannien und den USA weiteren Zulauf, während Bands in Motorradjacken wie The Clash und The Ramones jugendliche Ängste in Drei-Akkord-Songs zum Ausdruck brachten. Der New Yorker Club CB GB präsentierte Bands wie Television und The Talking Heads, die mit schrägen Stimmen und schlecht sitzenden Anzügen für Aufmerksamkeit sorgten, während Deborah Harry von Blondie das Publikum mit schwülen Songs und Stiletto-Stiefeln faszinierte.

Egal, ob man der New Yorker Punk-Szene nacheiferte oder mit The Grateful Dead auf den Aussteigertrip ging: Die Mode bot den Menschen mehr denn je die Freiheit, ihren eigenen Stil zu finden.

Above: *Hathaway, 1973*

# La mode en marge

par Laura Schooling

Au début des années 1970, le mouvement pour la paix qui avait marqué la fin de la décennie précédente est gangrené de pessimisme. Lorsque les soldats rentrent finalement du Vietnam en 1973, la plupart des Américains ont perdu leurs illusions et leur confiance dans le gouvernement. Des changements sociaux positifs sont pourtant dans l'air, grâce à l'ampleur prise par les mouvements militant pour les droits civiques et les droits des femmes. Tandis que certains luttent pour retrouver un semblant de normalité au milieu de ce chaos politique et culturel, d'autres sont emportés par cet élan et exigent une révolution, quel qu'en soit le prix. La mode fait preuve d'une égale duplicité, le courant dominant jouant la continuité dans la nuance et les courants marginaux brûlant de fantaisie et d'esprit révolutionnaire.

Le tout jeune magazine *Rolling Stone* donne une visibilité nationale aux héros du jour, à leur musique, mais aussi à leur garde-robe, qui contribue alors tout autant à leur succès. L'année 1970 voit aussi la déliquescence de la folie psychédélique qui avait connu son apogée dans les années 1960, en même temps que deux génies exubérants succombent aux excès de l'époque. Jimi Hendrix et Janis Joplin, morts d'overdose à quelques mois d'intervalle, étaient les icônes fantastiques du style psychédélique, avec leurs cheveux sauvages, leurs accumulations de perles, leurs longs gilets à glands, leurs vestes en velours, leurs manches gigot et ces tissus de toutes couleurs et textures. De façon plus discrète, les blousons en daim et les chapeaux à larges bords de Bob Dylan ou la raie au milieu et les jupes en vachette de Joni Mitchell reflètent l'esthétique *folk*. Les Beatles se séparent en 1970 et John Lennon devient inséparable de Yoko Ono. Les deux amants, qui portent de longues tuniques blanches identiques ou rien du tout, inaugurent une nouvelle tendance : le couple sosie. Les coupes de cheveux masculine et féminine se rapprochent jusqu'à atteindre une longueur moyenne unisexe, comme en témoignent les photos des Wings de Paul et Linda McCartney. Mais personne ne porte mieux l'androgynie que David Bowie, qui présente en 1972 son nouvel alter ego, Ziggy Stardust. Sur scène, avec ses allures d'ange bisexué, son maquillage outrancier et ses combinaisons moulantes et scintillantes, il prépare le grand public à l'explosion, proche, du mouvement gay.

Sur la couverture de son album *Pin Ups*, en 1973, Bowie pose avec Twiggy, qui se souviendra de cette séance comme d'un des moments les plus excitants de sa carrière. Le mannequin vedette des années 1960 a officiellement pris sa retraite au début de la nouvelle décennie et laissé la place à une moisson de nouveaux visages : Margaux Hemingway, Lauren Hutton et Beverly Johnson, premier mannequin noir à faire la Une de *Vogue*. La tendance, déclinée selon diverses représentations de la femme, est aux jeunes Américaines accessibles, de l'ingénue aux yeux immenses à la femme d'affaires. Si le clinquant et le glamour s'affichent dans les concerts de rock, les modèles des magazines n'en restent pas moins guindés et fades.

La saharienne lancée par Yves Saint Laurent en 1968 est toujours portée et largement copiée en 1973, mais rares sont les autres piliers de la mode des années

1960 à avoir survécu au changement de décennie. La minijupe jadis omniprésente a été remplacée par le short moulant, qui révèle autant les cuisses et permet de s'adonner librement à la danse, au patin à roulettes, ou même à la lutte contre le crime, comme le démontre magistralement Wonder Woman dans la série du même nom diffusée entre 1976 et 1979. En velours, en jean ou en alu, les *hot pants* se portent avec des bottes à talons carrés ou des sabots compensés pour allonger encore un peu plus la jambe. Dans le même temps, l'ourlet des jupes redescend sous le genou (midi) et même jusqu'au sol (maxi). Les pantalons à pattes d'éléphant passent avec succès du mouvement hippie à la mode urbaine du disco et du funk. En jeans ou en combinaison, les coupes sont aussi près du corps que possible au niveau des hanches pour s'élargir exagérément autour des chevilles.

Les couturiers français et italiens règnent toujours en maîtres, mais les créateurs américains construisent aussi leur empire. Halston est salué pour ses magnifiques robes flottantes et drapées au début de la décennie avant de devenir le chouchou d'égéries du disco comme Bianca Jagger ou Jerry Hall. Calvin Klein conçoit sa marque comme un style de vie. Avec le photographe Helmut Newton, il met autant l'accent sur le corps que sur les vêtements et vend la sexualité en même temps que ses lignes modernes et ses couleurs neutres. Ralph Lauren surfe sur le succès de sa griffe — notamment de ses cravates exubérantes — et crée une ligne pour femmes. Le mouvement pour les droits des femmes atteint son apogée et il s'agit de constituer une garde-robe compatible avec les nouveaux pouvoirs auxquels elles peuvent prétendre. Suivant l'exemple de vedettes porteuses de pantalons comme Katharine Hepburn, les créateurs de mode cherchent à proposer des vêtements à la fois élégants et adaptés aux activités d'une femme indépendante. C'est Ralph Lauren qui popularise le détournement des vêtements masculins pour les femmes en 1977, à l'image des costumes portés par Diane Keaton dans *Annie Hall*. Mais Lauren et Klein se sont surtout distingués en inaugurant une des tendances les plus rentables et durables du monde de la mode : le jean de créateur.

Le jean sert à confectionner tout, des sacs aux coussins, pour tous, du cow-boy à l'étudiante. La tendance au confort et à la décontraction atteint de nouveaux sommets avec l'avènement du pantalon en velours côtelé, qui transforme la mode masculine. Souvent décliné dans des coloris automnaux, il sert à tailler aussi bien les pantalons de tous les jours que des costumes trois pièces plus cérémonieux. Ce style est très bien porté par le personnage de Jack Tripper dans la série télévisée *Vivre à trois*, créée en 1977, tandis que le propriétaire M. Furley, arbore avec malice des ensembles costume cravate plus exubérants.

Entre 1970 et 1977, le grand public américain prend exemple sur la charmante femme active qu'incarne Mary Tyler Moore dans la série éponyme. Son style évolue du tailleur sage à des panoplies comportant manteau en mouton retourné, foulards, tuniques et les si seyantes robes portefeuille de Diane von Furstenberg. Mais personne n'a autant fait évoluer le vêtement « de bureau » que Giorgio Armani, qui façonne sa légende en créant des costumes androgynes pour les femmes et des coupes sobres pour les hommes. Il aborde la mode avec un état d'esprit d'artisan tailleur et dépasse tous les engouements avec son style propre, ajusté et pourtant décontracté.

Parallèlement à ce courant majoritaire, quelques anticonformistes engendrent dès le début des années 1970 le concept de «style personnel», qui marie fripes rétro, trouvailles de surplus militaires et vêtements de confection moins coûteux. À la fin de la décennie, les avant-gardistes de la mode étaient davantage connus pour leur personnalité que parce qu'ils avaient le dernier «must». Tout le monde porte jeans et T-shirts et trouve dans les boutiques des créateurs émergents les différentes inspirations qui nourrissent une nouvelle liberté vestimentaire. Geoffrey Beene plébiscite les lignes nettes et déconseille l'accumulation d'accessoires, Laura Ashley vulgarise la simplicité victorienne et Agnès b. crée des standards français d'une élégance discrète. Quelles que soient les influences, l'individualisme domine le style.

Lorsque le disco arrive, le punk sur les talons, l'ambiguïté vestimentaire n'est plus de mise. En 1974, le scandale du Watergate fait encore vaciller un peu plus la confiance de l'opinion américaine dans la Maison Blanche et, en 1975, Margaret Thatcher devient la première femme Premier ministre britannique. Les deux pays sont en profonde récession, le chômage et le mécontentement enflent, en particulier dans les classes laborieuses. L'Amérique tente de surmonter le marasme en se jetant à corps perdu dans les excès sémillants du disco. Dans *La Fièvre du Samedi soir*, présenté sur les écrans en 1977, John Travolta se fraye avec sa démarche chaloupée un passage sur la piste de danse illuminée d'une boîte de nuit. Il est vêtu d'un costume blanc très ajusté, au plus grand plaisir des femmes moulées dans des combinaisons pantalon en lycra ou drapées dans des robes dos nu et l'Amérique réclame à corps et à cris des vêtements qui scintilleront sous les boules à facettes. Le Studio 54 ouvre la même année à New York et devient l'épicentre de la décadence *seventies*, illustrée de façon spectaculaire par l'entrée de Bianca Jagger perchée sur un cheval blanc mené par un homme nu au corps peint. La tendance n'est plus à la subtilité mais à la surenchère. Cravates larges comme des serviettes de table, chaussures compensées, boucles d'oreilles qui viennent chatouiller l'épaule, cheveux emplumés, boucles de ceinture massives : tout ce qui peut être accentué l'est, de l'habillement aux attributs physiques qu'il couvre.

De l'autre côté de l'Atlantique, Johnnie Rotten et les Sex Pistols chantent l'absence d'avenir, «no future», et font voler en éclat toute conception établie de la mode et du conformisme en déchirant ou tailladant leurs vêtements, en dressant leurs cheveux et en ornant leurs jeans et cuirs sombres de symboles anarchistes. À leur grand dépit, leurs fans puis les millions de jeunes assoiffés de liberté récupèrent ces tentatives d'indépendance et les changent en bréviaire de l'*anti-establishment*, créant l'uniforme du parfait contestataire. Vivienne Westwood marque la mode punk d'une empreinte indélébile avec l'image de la Reine d'Angleterre une épingle à nourrice dans le nez.

Le punk prolifère dans tout le Royaume-Uni et les États-Unis quand des groupes de blousons noirs comme les Clash ou les Ramones convertissent la jeunesse aux mélodies rudimentaires. Le CBGB club de New York lance des groupes comme Television ou les Talking Heads, leur chant bancal et leurs costumes mal coupés, tandis que Blondie, alias Deborah Harry, captive ses admirateurs avec sa voix sensuelle et ses bottines à talon aiguille. Que l'on se jette dans la foule d'un concert punk à New York ou que l'on ondule sur les envolées de Grateful Dead, la mode offre en ce temps-là à chacun la liberté de suivre son rythme intime.

# Riviera Brings Fashion to Sunsensor™

### Hurry up sunshine! Fashion glasses...they turn darker as the sun turns brighter

Provocative! Intriguing! And superbly practical! "Sunsensor"™ lenses adjust to all light conditions...quickly, smoothly. Styled to match the life you lead. Fashion drama...available at fine stores everywhere... and exclusive styling from Riviera.

## *Riviera*®

295 Fifth Avenue, New York, N.Y. 10016   California   Toronto

*Riviera, 1974*

▶ *Cool-Ray Polaroid Sunglasses, 1970*

# Our sunglasses have a way of making a girl look great. Even after she takes them off.

Most people buy a pair of sunglasses because they think they look good in them. And they usually do.

In the store.

But out in the sun, it's a different story.

They squint.

With brand new sunglasses on, they squint. (And it's pretty hard for a girl to look her best with her nose wrinkled up and her eyes half shut.)

But you really can't expect much more from ordinary sunglasses. They just aren't designed to cut out reflected glare the way Cool-Ray Polaroid Sunglasses are.

Because the exclusive Polaroid lens is designed to act like an optical filter. It screens out the blinding glare reflected off water, sand, or just about anything else.

So, since you don't have to squint all day behind a pair of Cool-Ray Polaroid Sunglasses, you'll look as good in the sun as you did inside when you bought them.

And, since you don't have to strain your eyes all day just to see, you'll look great even after you take them off.

Which is usually just in time for an eight o'clock date.

This picture is kind of a copout.

In real life, the guy's hair would be matted down from the helmet. The chick would be your woman instead of a New York model. And you'd be eating exhaust from a bus somewhere instead of grooving in far out fields. However the Landlubbers are real; and they are mildly, but honestly transcendent.

Jeans and other gear, wherever they sell hip clothes to hip people. Sure, we'll tell you where.
Write Landlubber
M. Hoffman & Co., Inc.
Boston Mass. 02114.

*Landlubber, 1970*

▶ *Male, 1971*

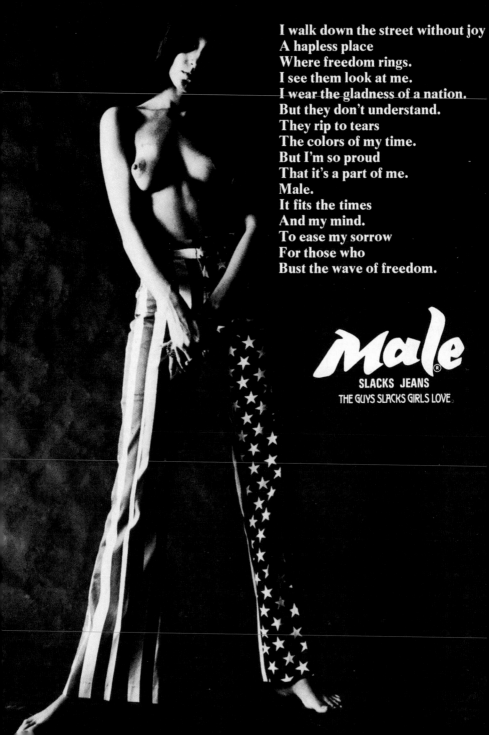

I walk down the street without joy
A hapless place
Where freedom rings.
I see them look at me.
I wear the gladness of a nation.
But they don't understand.
They rip to tears
The colors of my time.
But I'm so proud
That it's a part of me.
Male.
It fits the times
And my mind.
To ease my sorrow
For those who
Bust the wave of freedom.

# Male

SLACKS JEANS
THE GUYS SLACKS GIRLS LOVE

MISS SPRINGMAID

SPRINGMAID OF THE MONTH

Miss Springmaid of the Month is Kathie McCarron.
The fabric (not the mini-over-bikini) is Springmaid.
Also makers of famous Springmaid sheets.

SPRINGS MILLS, INC., 104 WEST 40TH ST., NEW YORK, N.Y. 10018.
FOR THE STORE NEAREST YOU, CALL ANY HOUR, ANY DAY AT NO TELEPHONE
CHARGE: (800) 243-6000. IN CONNECTICUT, CALL (800) 942-0655.

*Springmaid, 1970*

# PANDORA

**Body Stripers!**

The big, bold, beautiful band-its!
Pandora's gala gang-up of knits in
purest 100% cotton. Outrageously
striped—tops (sizes s m l) to bottoms
(sizes 5 to 15) left to right—'look ma'
no-sleeves pullover about $5,
belt'n chain, flip-flare skirt $8, U-neck
tunic & dress $6, runaway pants $8,
shifty white collar girl $8. For your
lucky stripe-a-match store, write
Pandora, Inc.,1407 Broadway, N.Y.1001?

*Pandora*®

Prices slightly higher west of the Rockies

*Pandora, 1970*

Levi's for Gals low rise flared jeans, about $11. He's wearing Levi's Sta-Prest® flared slacks, about $14. Levi's for Gals is a division of Levi Strauss & Co. San Francisco. The words "Levi's" and "Sta-Prest" are registered trademarks.

**Have you ever had a bad time in Levi's?**

# Tall Stories from Thom McAn.

Sometime, on a rainy afternoon, someone will ask you to read to them.
And that's the time to wear Tall Stories. They're soft, rich suede
and Carnaby heels. In plum, rust, sand and slate. $19.99.

Fairytales will never seem silly again. Thom McAn

THE SILKEN LOOK
SPICED BY GEOFFREY BEENE

# Suddenly, the suit has exciting new possibilities!

For a long time now, the role of the suit has been changing.

You've seen the signs.

Men used to wear suits strictly for business, and save the "livelier" clothes for weekends.

But today's fashion lets you wear bolder suits everywhere—to country club as readily as to business meeting.

Yes, the boundaries have blurred, and the scope of the suit has widened.

And now, from Hammonton, comes an idea that expands a suit's horizons even further!

New designs that open up many new options.

Suddenly, your entire approach to fashion can be more varied and exciting ...more fun!

*eoffrey Beene, 1974* ◀

*Hammonton, 1974*

# The kind of guy who uses it doesn't need it.

**Pub Cologne.**

After Shave, After Shave Balm, Deodorant Spray, too.

# "Peace in '70" for $2.75

Show how you feel.
Get your "Peace in '70" Sweatshirts.
A top quality, shrink-proof Sweatshirt.
In dove white and love red.
Long and short sleeves available in S,M,L,XL.
From the man who bottles Coca-Cola to you for only $2.75.
Wear it in peace. And while you're at it,
have an ice-cold Coca-Cola. It's the real thing.

**Love's A Little Cover is a sheer, smooth makeup
that covers so well, you'll look fresh and soft even in daylight.**

Love's A Little Cover* evens out your skin tone.
Love's A Little Cover covers even minor skin imperfections.
Love's A Little Cover comes in ten subtle shades from light to deep.
It makes you look so fresh and soft,
you won't have to worry about the harsh light of day.

**Love Cosmetics by Menley & James.**

THIS IS LOVE IN 1972

# Royal Shield naturals lead a fuller life

Never has there been a hair style so easy to care for. But even the simplest things need some care. Make it special. Royal Shield natural products help you make the most of it. Hair actually blossoms with shimmering new body and fullness.

You not only get the look and feel of **more hair** but Royal Shield's gentle protein-rich formula gives it the sheen of **better** hair. If you've decided natural is the way to go. Then take Royal Shield along.

**HOW DOES PROTEIN WORK?**
Protein is nature's own restorer. Tiny protein molecules penetrate the hair shaft, uniting with the structure of the hair to become part of the shaft itself. Naturally makes hair stronger. Anytime you use one of the Royal Shield products (for control or sheen, conditioning, or dressing) you add new life and lustre, obedient new fullness with each application.

Isn't it time you turned your natural into everything it could be?

Royal Shield Blow-Out Creme makes any natural almost twice as big. And you do it by yourself. Easy and gentle to use. Protein enriched for lasting results.

with protein

ROYAL SHIELD

*Royal Shield, 1972*

▶ *Afro Sheen, 1971*   ▶▶ *Posner, 1971*

# SHADES OF *Africa*

From the Great Continent comes inspiration for the new look in lipstick. Sensuous shades with an African accent to drench your mouth in never-before-colors.

From the high plateaus in East Africa comes Nairobi Beige—soft, cool and subtle.

From the dazzling Gold Coast comes Ghana Red—bold, bright and beautiful.

From Africa's plumage comes Tanzania Flamingo, the pink of beauty.

Fifteen shimmering shades that put Africa on your lips and new excitement in your look.

*Posner Laboratories, Inc., Corona, N.Y. 11368*

**LIP DAZZLERS:**
GHANA RED
LIP SHEEN (wear it over any color for an added dimension of shimmer)

**SHADES OF COOL:**
NAIROBI BEIGE
NAIROBI BEIGE-FROST
NIGERIAN COCOA
NIGERIAN COCOA-FROST
CONGO COFFEE
CONGO COFFEE-FROST

**TROPICAL TONES:**
IVORY COAST MAHOGANY
IVORY COAST MAHOGANY-FROST
TANZANIA FLAMINGO-FROST

Fabric for gele from Kenberry

POSNER

CUSTOM BLENDS
AFRICAN LIPSTICK COLLECTION

Who can say "no" to a gorgeous brunette?

Black can be as beautiful as you make it... if you make it happen with the magic of Loving Care.® It's the gentle haircoloring. Washes away the gray while it enriches your natural hair color.

It's different. Nothing to mix. No peroxide, so it can't really change your natural shade.

Easy to do, too. It's a lotion. Just pour it on. Even has its own wonderful conditioner to keep your hair shiny.

So you can be as beautifully black on the outside as you are on the inside.

And you can't get any more natural than that.

Loving Care® — the gentle hair color from Clairol for natural, pressed and relaxed hair.

# Get the Upsy-Daisy...

## It's FREE! with Adorn!

**Adorn** SELF-STYLING HAIR SPRAY

Free UPSY DAISY

**It fluffs!**   **It puffs!**   **It curls!**

The Upsy-Daisy makes beautiful hairdos easy—and it's free with Adorn! Build a smashing style with The Upsy-Daisy—then hold it—with Self-Styling Adorn. See all the exciting hairdos in the styling book. It's all free with Adorn in the exclusive touch-top container. Get it now! Self-Styling Adorn hairspray.

## Announcing the best-dressed men in America.

You're looking at a revolution.

The most influential men in America are breaking out of their socks—out of their old, blah, boring, one-color, no-style socks.

At Interwoven/Esquire Socks, we saw it coming all the way. That's why we make the great fashion socks that are making it happen.

In lots of great colors and lengths. All in the first Ban-Lon® pattern socks ever made. They feel softer and fit better than any sock you've ever worn.

That's why we dress the best-dressed men in America. Or anywhere.

Another fine product of Kayser-Roth

**Be kind to your behind**

# HotPants.

After a long season of hisses
and boos, bare your legs.
The boys deserve a break.
So do you. That's what
HotPants are all about.
Movement. Freedom.
Action. And the boys will
be cheering. HotPants
from Wards. They're like a shot
to the ego.

Open a Wards "Charg-All"
account. It makes shopping
simpler in our store or
catalog.

Butterfly printed washable acetate jersey. Tunic with dog collar neckline. Red with navy or navy with red. Junior petites 5 to 13. $13. • All cotton midriff outfit. HotPants have front button detail, patch pocket and contrasting cuffs. Navy with white, white with navy or burgundy with white. 6 to 16. $7.

**Introducing Encron Strialine.
The first slub polyester.
It puts a little texture in your life,
for a change.**

Look at the look of the fabric by Knit-Away. It's unplain. Total texture. What you can't see is the way these pants of Encron Strialine polyester perform. They're easy care and firm about keeping in shape.

Available at fine department & specialty stores everywhere. Contact Farah Manufacturing Co. Inc., P.O. Box 9519, El Paso, Texas 79985, for the store nearest you.

**The slacks
by Farah.**

**ENKA**

Enka, 1974 ◄

Pg's, 1975

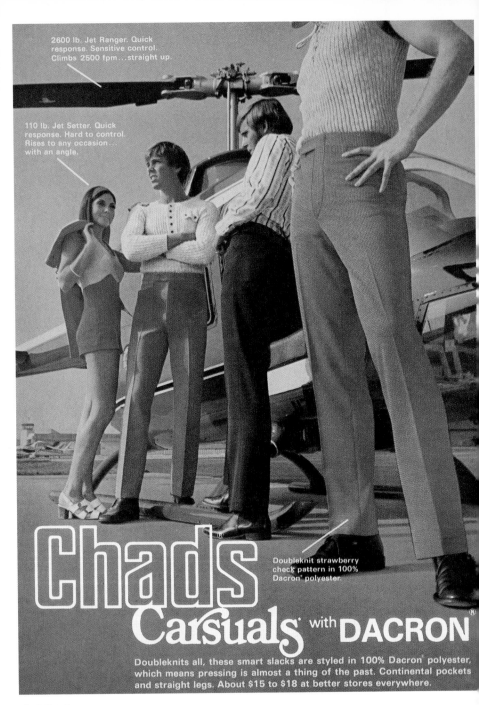

2600 lb. Jet Ranger. Quick response. Sensitive control. Climbs 2500 fpm...straight up.

110 lb. Jet Setter. Quick response. Hard to control. Rises to any occasion... with an angle.

Doubleknit strawberry check pattern in 100% Dacron polyester.

# Chads
## Carsuals with DACRON®

Doubleknits all, these smart slacks are styled in 100% Dacron polyester, which means pressing is almost a thing of the past. Continental pockets and straight legs. About $15 to $18 at better stores everywhere.

*Chads Casuals, 1971*

# Sears Give-n'-Take II knit slacks.
# When it's your move, it's their move.

Here are the slacks that will bend over backward... or forward or sideways... to keep you comfortable. They can't help it. That's the way they're made. The 100% Trevira® polyester double knit goes every way you do, but never goes out of shape. That goes for the new stretch Ban-Rol® waistband, too. What's more, these are Perma-Prest® fabric slacks, so after they go in a washer and come out of a tumble dryer they're all ready to go again. Choose Give-n'-Take II double knit slacks in Trim Regular or Full Cut models at most Sears, Roebuck and Co. stores or through the regular or Big and Tall catalogs.

**Give-n'-Take II double knit slacks and all that goes with them at Sears The-Men's-Store**

Sears | The·Men's·Store | KINGS ROAD shop

**This is the tag you should look for even before you check the price tag.**

**You'll find it on this body suit by Diplomat.**

The Herculon II* tag. It tells you what no price tag can.

That Diplomat is no Johnny-come-lately. They've long been a pace setter. A perennial fashion innovator. And proud of the reputation they've built.

The Herculon II tag tells you Diplomat doesn't mind working a little harder to maintain that reputation. Putting in the extra effort it may take to meet Herculon II standards. So this body suit at about $15.00 doesn't come out looking like anybody else's body suit. At any price.

**TUA MARKETING, INC.**
1345 Avenue of the Americas, New York, New York 10019

*Trademark of Hercules Incorporated

Strike up the band. Here's Mach II in a patriotic mood. A red-white-and-blue shirt featuring the extra-longpoint collar. The slacks, a solid complement in basic white. Mach II. A slim and tapered look that's carried out in a whole new line of sport and dress shirts from ➤**Arrow**➤

A right-angular state of mind. Mach II.

# CHANEL

erfume in the classic bottle from 8.50 to 400., Eau de Chanel from 7.00 to 20.00, Eau de Cologne from 4.00 to 20.00, Spray Perfume and Spray Cologne each 6.0

*Chanel, 1973*

a
whole
new way
of
walking

**PADRINO**
marshmallows, platforms and down to earth fashions

**SMERLING IMPORTS, INC.** 350 Fifth Avenue (Suite 7419) New York, N.Y. 10001

*Tempos, 1973* ◄

*Padrino, 1974*

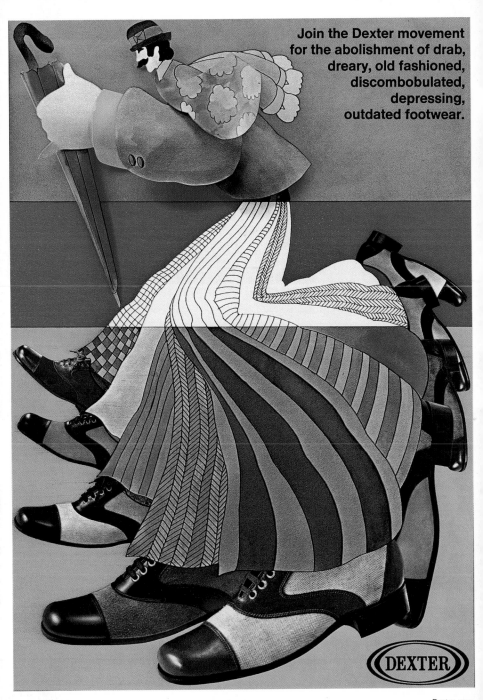

Join the Dexter movement for the abolishment of drab, dreary, old fashioned, discombobulated, depressing, outdated footwear.

DEXTER

# Congratulations.
## Sears just cut corners on
# The-Comfort-Shirt.

Actually, we had the corners
rounded. Not a lot. Just enough so
The-Comfort-Shirt with the long-
pointed-collar finally has competition.
Either way you get the super-
comfortable C-Band® collar,
tapered body, extra long shirttails,
and a Perma-Prest® fabric blended
from Fortrel® polyester and cotton.
Price? Let's just say you won't
have to cut corners to buy a few,
along with gotogether ties.
The-Comfort-Shirt.
In most Sears, Roebuck and Co.
stores, and through the Catalog.
In both long and short sleeves. And in
all kinds of prints, stripes and solids.

**The-Comfort-Shirt
and all that goes with it at
Sears The-Men's-Store**

*SUPPLIER FOR THE U.S. OLYMPIC TEAM*

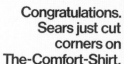

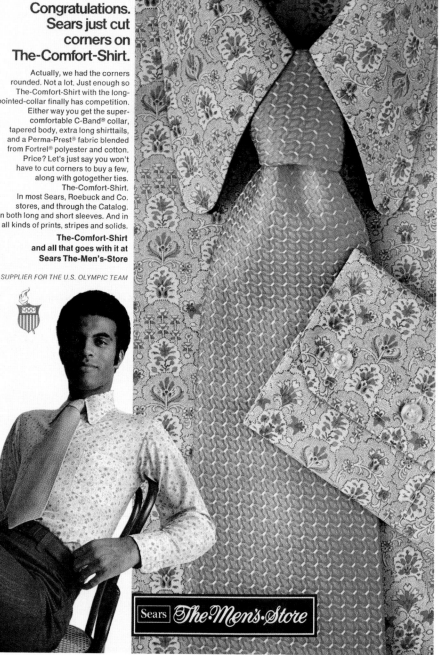

**Sears** *The·Men's·Store*

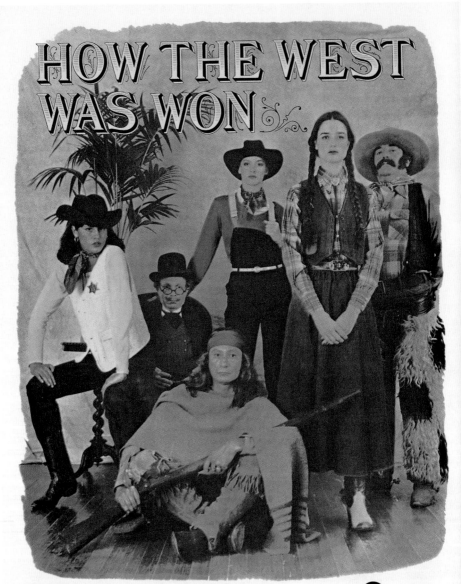

# HOW THE WEST WAS WON

Out of the West comes a look that is changing the way America dresses. It's bright, bold, sassy and sweet. And, the Gap's got it. Straight leg denims, bright knits, earth tone vests in burlap or suede, and the new look in overalls. Discover the fashion look of the West at The Gap. You'll be glad you did.

© The Gap Stores, Inc. 1978

SAN FRANCISCO BAY AREA, LOS ANGELES, SAN DIEGO, STOCKTON, FRESNO.

*The Gap, 1978*

▶ *London Fog, 197*

# Play it again, London Fog.

It's not the same old story. London Fog® has updated the classic trenchcoat look with Imaginit*—a new woven fabric with the stretch, shape and wrinkle-resistance you've always wanted. Plus the protection of London Fog's own water-repellent formula. On that you can rely.

## LONDON FOG®
### lets you laugh at the weather

# Here's Johnny!

*. . . great mixer that he is, with his sport duo that blends polyester for easy care, finespun wool for a soft touch and linen for a crisp, summer look. For complete coordination, add the Johnny Carson® shirts and ties especially designed for the duo. See it all at fine stores throughout the United States and Canada.*

## Johnny Carson Apparel, Inc.

For name of nearest dealer, write to 2020 Elmwood Ave., Buffalo, N.Y. 142
Canadian residents, write to 637 Lakeshore Blvd. W., Toronto 2B, Ontario

Johnny's Sport Duo is
61% polyester, 28% wool worsted
and 11% linen.

*photographed by Howell Conant
at Tres Vidas, Acapulco, Mexico*

PBM gives the punch of plaid to the great American wools.

Pick a plaid this year. A bigger, bolder, brighter one. A plaid by PBM. And definitely a wool plaid—because wool takes to color beautifully and holds its shape likewise. The plaids shown here, by J.P. Stevens. Fashion selection by the American Wool Council.

**PBM**®

PURE WOOL

# PANDORA

**The newsmakers!** The ego-builders!
The super 'Singles' that mate plaidly,
perfectly, smashingly! The live-a-lot glen
plaid in 100% Acrilan® acrylic, halter
jumper about $19, trousers $18. Acrilan®
ribbed turtle top $10, white collar 'n
cuffed bodysuit $15. Sizes 5 to 15.
Pandora Industries, Inc.,
1407 Broadway, N.Y. 10018.

*Pandora®*

*Pandora, 1972*

► *Sears, 1973*

# PANT DRESSING

Dressing.
As easy as one, two, three.

Three pieces.
All sweater ribbed.
Cardigan jacket. White collared
top. And pants.

All 100% polyester doubleknit.
Machine wash-and-dryable.

Exclusively ours.
Under $36.
In misses sizes 8 to 18.

At most Sears, Roebuck and Co.
larger stores.

You'll find lots more
where this came from.
In our Dress Department.
Come try on.

My "Parfum"
... Inspired and dedicated
to women of Love
Aldo Gucci

Rare jewels of the world

**HARRY WINSTON** INC.

718 Fifth Ave., New York, N.Y. 10019  Paris and Geneva

# It took a Black company to come up with a wig for the Black woman.

It's about time, isn't it?

Today you can buy lipstick, nail polish, make-up creams and powders made just for you.

Today you can buy hair conditioners, eye colorings, shampoos and hair sprays made just for you. (And we thank you for buying so many from us.)

But why can't you buy a wig made just for you? You can.

Because we went to the people who make Kanekalon—one of the world's largest manufacturers of wig fibers—and asked them to create a fiber specifically for a Black woman's wig.

The result is Afrylic—a high-quality modacrylic fiber that is specially processed to give your wig just the right body . . . just the right curl . . . just the right sheen. In fact, Afrylic looks so natural, we've created three different wig styles to choose from. And all of these stretch wigs are wash-and-wear for easy care.

You'll find our exciting new line of Afrylic Wigs at your beauty salon, wig shop, or department store. It's been a long time coming, but it's finally here:

A wig that was created to make the Black woman even more beautiful.

## Summit's Afrylic*Wigs

*Processed exclusively for Summit by the makers of Kanekalon

AFRYLIC AFRO $25.00

AFRYLIC SHAG $30.00

AFRYLIC CURLY $27.50

*Summit's Afrylic Wigs, 1971*

▶ *Ultra Sheen, 1970*

Above all ... Phoenix Clothes

*Phoenix Clothes, 1974*

▶ *Dr. Scholl's, 1974*

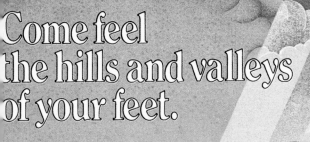

# Come feel the hills and valleys of your feet.

Come rest your feet in the hollows
and the rises.

Experience the coolness of polished beechwood
against the warmth of bare skin.

Feel the little mound we call the toe-grip,
that helps you turn mere steps into a beautiful
toning and awakening for your legs.

Celebrate the sole, for it is the most sensitive
thing of all.

Scholl, the original Exercise Sandal.

Feeling is believing.

Pierre Cardin, 1971

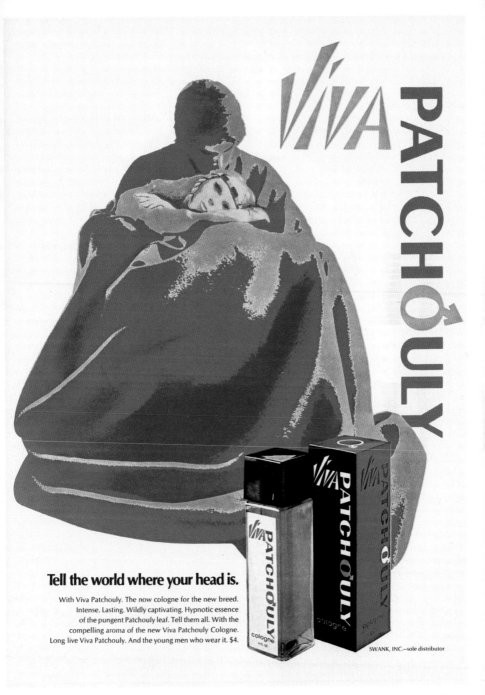

# VIVA PATCHOULY

## Tell the world where your head is.

With Viva Patchouly. The now cologne for the new breed.
Intense. Lasting. Wildly captivating. Hypnotic essence
of the pungent Patchouly leaf. Tell them all. With the
compelling aroma of the new Viva Patchouly Cologne.
Long live Viva Patchouly. And the young men who wear it. $4.

SWANK, INC.—sole distributor

*Viva Patchouly, 1971*

See what a little Hubba Hubba does for you.

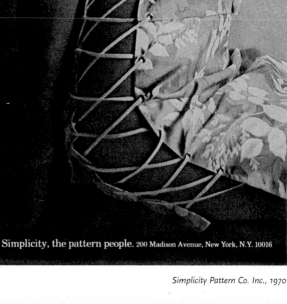

# All of us have the urge, but not all of us have the nerve.

If you want to look different these days you have a choice.

#1, you can look ridiculous.

#2, you can look like you came off an assembly line.

Well, we think the secret to looking different is really being yourself, because that never goes out of style.

And that brings us to #3, the perfect answer: a Simplicity pattern.

We have our people all over the country, all over the world for that matter, reporting in to us so we can create the latest fashions for you.

But it takes one more person to make them exactly what you want.

That's you.

Because you're the one who says "it should be a jumpsuit, in crushed velvet with fur cuffs." Not us.

If you'd like to keep up with all the latest excitement in the world of fashions, just keep up with our Simplicity Fashion News.

All the fashions are photographed beautifully in color.

And another beautiful thing is that the Fashion News is free. So make sure you get your copy as soon as you can. With a Simplicity pattern, instead of showing you have a lot of nerve, you'll show you have a lot of taste.

Simplicity.
Being yourself never goes out of style.

Simplicity, the pattern people. 200 Madison Avenue, New York, N.Y. 10016

# Turn Yourself On to A

### Vivacious Violet Eyes

SHEER FOUNDATION— "Bare Bronze" •
BEAUTY BLUSH—"Plum Rose" • ALL
AGLOW—"Luscious Plum" • TRANSGLO—
"Deep" • EYE SHADOW DUO—"Vivacious
Violet", "Lilac Lustre" • LIPSTICK—"Ripest Red".

### Dare To Be Different Eyes

"Bare Bronze" SHEER FOUNDATION was smoothed on to even complexion.

TRANSGLO PRESSED POWDER "Deep" was puffed on to set and reduce shine without changing foundation tones.

BEAUTY BLUSH "Plum Rose" was brushed toward outer lines of cheek bone only. Model's natural line did not need further definition for highlight or color.

"Sea Aqua" EYE SHADOW was stroked boldly on eyelids; "Aqua Pearl" followed the crease and was blended up toward outer eye. To finish the look—a light stroke of "Sea Aqua" along inner brow line to brow peak.

FASHION FAIR EYELINER CAKE was applied very close to upper lash line, with a fine line at outer edges of lower lashes.

"Bark Black" MASCARA (several applications) gave added thickness and length to lashes.

"Soft Black" BROW PENCIL completed this Dare To Be Different look.

LIP BALANCER evened lip tones and then just a touch of "Bashful Burgundy" LIPSTICK.

*Fashion Fair Cosmetics, 1972*

# New Facial Makeup

## The *Fashion Fair* Collection

## Choice of Ebony Fashion Fair Models

You, too, can be as strikingly lovely as the beautiful Black models everyone admires. Coming your way soon—created just for you—is the brand new FASHION FAIR COLLECTION, a complete line of distinctive and elegant facial cosmetics that have been carefully blended and then tested by models...the real makeup experts. For every woman who wants to achieve the ultimate in beauty perfection, FASHION FAIR offers everything from purifying masques and luxurious deep cleanser to specially-blended foundations, powders and blushers to heavenly eye shadow duos.

Watch for our ads announcing when the FASHION FAIR COLLECTION will be in your city. We're on our way!

### Nude 'n' Natural Eyes

"Honey Amber" SHEER FOUNDATION gives just the necessary warmth to begin this natural look. "Spiced Orange" ALL AGLOW was slicked along and slightly below cheek bones, then blended. TRANSGLO "Fair" was applied lightly to reduce shine . . . but not the glow.

Too small eyes were brought out boldly with "Bone Pearl" on lower half of lid; a wide stroke of "Bold Brown" follows along the crease and is peaked at middle of eye. That's the drama of this look. "Bone Pearl" between brow line and crease adds final highlight.

"Brown/Black" EYELINER follows. We used a fairly strong line, both along upper lash line and below lower lashes.

To add soft fringe, "Bark Black" MASCARA was brushed on upper and lower lashes. "Soft Black" BROW PENCIL defines brow line boldly, but not harshly.

LIP BALANCER evened lip tones . . . then "Barest Beige" LIPSTICK for just a hint of color but lots of gloss.

After eye shadow application, all models wear FASHION FAIR'S EYE ACCENT COLLECTION.

### Simply Sensational Eyes

SHEER FOUNDATION—"Copper Blaze"• BEAUTY BLUSH —"Bronze Blush"• TRANSGLO OIL ABSORBENT PRESSED POWDER "Deep"—• EYESHADOW DUOS—"Jade Green" "Jeweled Jade", "Bold Brown", "Bone Pearl" • LIPSTICK— "Orange Ole".

### Tenderly Tinted Eyes

SHEER FOUNDATION—"Honey Amber" • ALL AGLOW— "Luscious Plum" • TRANSGLO OIL ABSORBENT PRESSED POWDER—"Deep" • EYE SHADOW DUOS—"Jade Green", "Jeweled Jade", "Bold Brown", "Bone Pearl" • LIP BALANCER • LIPSTICK—"Cinnamon Crush".

Send 25¢ (for postage and handling) and we'll send you the beautiful Fashion Fair Collection Brochure. Fashion Fair Cosmetics, Division of Johnson Publishing Company, 820 So. Michigan Ave., Chicago, Ill. 60605.

*The tie for the shirt by Hathaway.*

# The sound of Jazz: Hathaway's Cabaret Plaid.

It's bold and beautiful! Like the vibrant tones from an Armstrong or Beiderbecke.
Syncopated checks over checks create real added dimension in this stunning
Cabaret Plaid, and the sheik, Rutland collar is a perfect set-up for a
contemporary bow tie. The shirt is a weave of Durable
Press polyester and cotton, priced at $16.00. For the store nearest you, write
C. F. Hathaway Company, Waterville, Maine 04901, a division of Warnaco, Inc.

## CABARET PLAID
### EXCLUSIVELY HATHAWAY

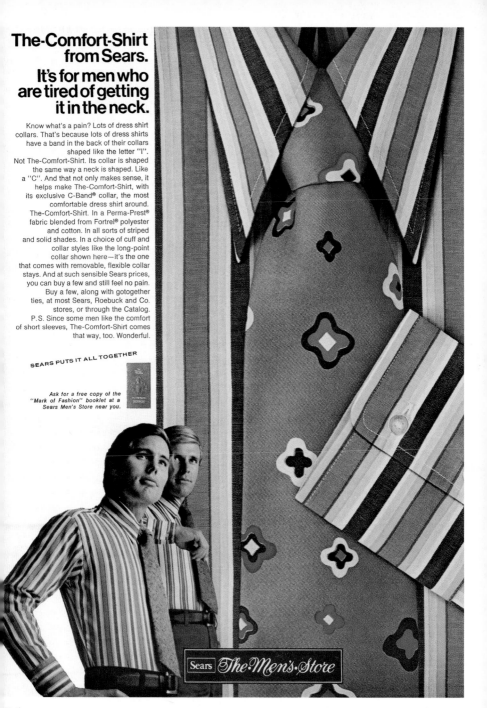

# The-Comfort-Shirt from Sears.
# It's for men who are tired of getting it in the neck.

Know what's a pain? Lots of dress shirt collars. That's because lots of dress shirts have a band in the back of their collars shaped like the letter "I". Not The-Comfort-Shirt. Its collar is shaped the same way a neck is shaped. Like a "C". And that not only makes sense, it helps make The-Comfort-Shirt, with its exclusive C-Band® collar, the most comfortable dress shirt around. The-Comfort-Shirt. In a Perma-Prest® fabric blended from Fortrel® polyester and cotton. In all sorts of striped and solid shades. In a choice of cuff and collar styles like the long-point collar shown here—it's the one that comes with removable, flexible collar stays. And at such sensible Sears prices, you can buy a few and still feel no pain. Buy a few, along with gotogether ties, at most Sears, Roebuck and Co. stores, or through the Catalog. P.S. Since some men like the comfort of short sleeves, The-Comfort-Shirt comes that way, too. Wonderful.

SEARS PUTS IT ALL TOGETHER

Ask for a free copy of the "Mark of Fashion" booklet at a Sears Men's Store near you.

Sears *The·Men's·Store*

Stop depending on someone else to lend you <u>her</u> sewing machine. Discover the heady new freedom of having your own. So you can sew up the kind of clothes <u>you</u> want, whenever you want. Discover The Independence Machines from Singer. They're a great group— priced for young purses. Take the <u>Fashion Mate</u>* zig-zag sewing machine by Singer (model 237). This portable sews both straight and zig-zag (perfect for knits). It sews buttons, buttonholes, embroiders, appliques All for just $88—including carrying case!

There's another Fashion Mate machine for $69.95. And remind your folks about the Singer 1-to-36 Credit Account. Choose your Independence Machine at your Singer Center now.

# The Independence Machine

Free at Singer: folder on making "Freedom Fashions"— like the appliqued outfit here. And for just $7.95 get the whole scoop on sewing in the SINGER* Sewing Book.

*What's new for tomorrow is at* SINGER *today.*

* A Trademark of THE SINGER COMP

# If you like this sport shirt, you're under thirty

The Patch Job by Manhattan®: 65% Kodel® polyester, 35% cotton

You've got your own ideas of what's fun in shirts. What looks good on you. And America's middle-age shirt companies just aren't making it. Therefore: Manhattan® U-30®—the first sport shirt collection designed expressly for the man under thirty. Pared-to-the-bone, shaped and tapered body with narrower arms. Longer point collars, deeper cuffs. Permanent press. U-30. More than a shirt. A life style—like this anti-establishment Patch Job, $9. At fine stores in U.S.A. and Canada.

**Manhattan®**
U-30. The Under-30 Shirt

## What to wear on Sunday
## when you won't be home till Monday.

You're on your own. Free to be yourself in everything you do or wear.

That's what Happy Legs is all about. We make things only for spirits like yours. No one else would dig the freedom and taste of our tops and pants. We cut and shape them only for long-legged bodies like yours. In junior sizes. Some day soon, like before next Sunday just go into a store that knows sportswear and pick out your own look from Happy Legs, Inc., 1407 Broadway, New York 10018, (212) 695-2255. A Spencer Company.

### Happy Legs
fits you, fits your life-style.

# Scrunch, stretch and be merry in Pants That Fit.

You've got a lot of things to take care of over the holidays. But not our pants. They almost take care of themselves.

They're wrinkle-resistant. Because they're Perma-Prest fabric of polyester doubleknit. So they bend when you bend. And then fall right back into shape.

They're trim without being tight. Pull-ons and fitted waists. In misses sizes 8-20 proportioned to your height. Terrific with Sears tops.

Come try on. At most Sears, Roebuck and Co. larger stores. Also in the catalog or by telephone to Catalog Shopping Service.

*Sears*
Pants    Fit™

Sears

# Avon brings you Christmas.

Your Avon Lady brings something wonderful—
and unique!—for every wonderful someone
you know. Deliciously feminine colognes
and manly aftershaves, in decanters worth keeping.
Jewelry—for Her and Him. And happy kids' things
of course. All ready for Christmas morning
in decorative cartons that just need a bow
and a gift card. When Avon brings you Christmas,
be ready with your gift list . . . and a smile.

# AVON

ROCKEFELLER PLAZA, NEW YORK. ©1971 AVON PRODUCTS, INC.

*Blackglama, 1973*

▶ *Vanity Fair, 1973*

Our kilt-edged quilt: a weightless puff that wraps you warm, skinside and out, in sumptuous nylon satin. The waffled quilting pattern is just one of our new untraditionals. Tapestry Green lined with Snow Jade (shown), Black with Wildfire, Brownstone with Buff. All endlessly machine wash-and-dryable. 8 to 18. About $40. Vanity Fair Mills, Inc., 640 Fifth Ave., New York, New York.

# VANITY FAIR

A company of **VF** corporation

Jantzen looks for
the carefree man.
With doubleknit jeans.

Look carefree even when you care.
Look for Jantzen 100% tailored doubleknit jeans. In solids,
patterns or stripes. About $20.
Casually matched with coordinating knit shirts. In
delicious colors like grapevine and blueberry. From $9.
Take it easy... Jantzen looks for you.

# Jantzen®

Wards. The unexpected.

MONTGOMERY
WARD

Miniature cable pattern in Dacron® polyester and cotton knit. Button front cardigan top, pull-on HotPants. Machine washable. Berry, brown or navy. 8 to 16. $12. • All nylon midriff. Elasticized puffy sleeves, shirred with elastic at neck, sleeves and midriff. Black, white, orangy-red, yellow or navy. S,M,L. $6. • Double knit Acrilan® acrylic HotPants. Elastic waistband. White, red, brown or black. 6 to 16. $4.

*Jantzen, 1972* ◄

*Montgomery Ward, 1971*

# Glow for the Holidays

To keep your looks as sparkling bright as the holiday season ahead, turn up your glow to a holiday intensity. Glisten your lips, your eyes, and your cheeks with Posner Custom Blends Cosmetics.

Posner Custom Blends won't fade, won't change color. They're specially formulated to be low-in-oils and right-in-color, so they stay fresh and natural all day long. Look for Posner Custom Blends Cosmetics at your favorite cosmetics counter or write: Posner Laboratories, Inc., Corona, N.Y. 11368.

**POSNER**
## CUSTOM BLENDS
### COSMETICS

*The Professional*

# Duke® STYLE CHART

**DUKE** has everything for the PERFECT Natural

*The Atom*    *The Taper*

*Watusi*    *Full Round*

**Duke.** SHAMPOO

**Duke** NATURAL EASY C

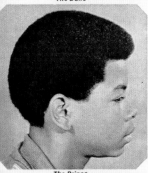
*The Duke*

*The Prince*

*The 'Fro*

*The Sportsman*

*The Flattop*

*Suave*

*The Executive*

**Supreme Beauty Products Co.**
820 So. Michigan Ave.
Chicago, Ill. 60605

For Enlarged Reprint of Duke
Chart Suitable For Window
or Wall Send $1.00.

*Private Eye*

*The Jet Setter*

*Blow-Up*

*New Natural*

*The Perfecto*

# I've found an inexpensive little dressmaker!

## Me.

Yes. Me. Suddenly I'm really getting great at sewing. Thanks to One Touch Sewing on the Golden Touch & Sew° machine by Singer. It really put easy sewing at my finger-tips. Even tricky patterns are for me, now. Take this number I'm wearing. Cinchy! One touch and I picked one of nine stretch stitches. (They have more "give" for slinky things!) Another touch and I could sew zig-zags. Even the bobbin winds at the push of a button!

The Singer 1 to 36° Credit Plan will help you get the machine of your choice, within your budget.

To make this dress: McCall's 3155, 100% woven polyester, 45" wide, 2.99 yd. At most Singer Sewing Centers.

# SINGER

*A Trademark of THE SINGER COMPANY

**The best double coverage on the court. Wigwam Socks and Converse All Stars.®**

Wigwam Socks and Converse All Stars. They work together for fit, feel, support, and comfort. From one end of the court to the other.

Wigwam Socks come high or low, in different styles and colors to match your All Stars.

Converse All Stars, high-cut or low, in smooth leather, suede or canvas, in your team colors. To match your Wigwams.

Put your best feet forward this season. Put them in Wigwam Socks and Converse All Stars.

**Wigwam Socks and Converse All Stars.**

# The Winner. Built by Converse.® Just for Sears.

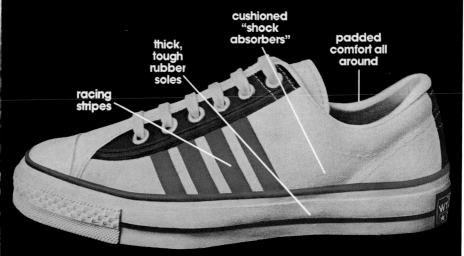

cushioned "shock absorbers"

thick, tough rubber soles

padded comfort all around

racing stripes

*Wigwam and Converse, 1974* ◄

*Sears, 1974*

# Now...pretty things come in Sunny Bunches. Only at Sears.

Color it new. Color it now. Color it just in time for Christmas.

The Sunny Bunch. Sears exclusive new collection of color coordinated clothes. All designed with a young girl's fancy in mind.

The Sunny Bunch. Easy care dresses, pants and tops in sizes 7-14, Pretty Plus sizes 8½-16½. Each with its own sweet character. Each with its own sunny style.

The Sunny Bunch. Color coordinated to make mixing and matching easy. And reasonably priced to make shopping more fun.

The Sunny Bunch. Pretty things to brighten her day. Only at Sears.

The Sunny Bunch™

**Sears**

©Sears, Roebuck and Co., 1978

Pretty things come in Sunny Bunches.

Styles and colors are representative of many in most larger Sears retail stores. Other items from The Sunny Bunch Collection are available in the Catalog.

# A LEGEND ON THE BLOCK NEEDS A LEGEND ON HIS JEANS.

He's conquered every fence, tree, and vacant lot on the block.

But when it comes to jeans, he's met his match: Levi's® Since 1850, pants with the Levi's "tab" on the back have shrugged off everything from bucking broncos to bicycle sprockets.

Look for Levi's Youthwear. In denim and corduroy, sizes 2 to 14.

You can spend a fortune trying to keep a legend in clothes. Or you can make every penny count. Like they did in the old days. With Levi's.

## Levi's
### YOUTHWEAR

QUALITY NEVER GOES OUT OF STYLE.

# If they could just stay young til their Carter's wear out.

Carter's sleepwear. Grownup looks for your little
girls. Easy-care fabrics for you. In polyester/cotton
and all cotton blends that wash easily and wear well...
because they're Carter's.

Sizes 3-6X from $6.00*    Sizes 7-14 from $5.50*

*Suggested retail prices

# LAZY BONES

REG. U.S. PAT. OFF. & CANADA. MADE IN U.S.A.

## TODAY'S SHOES FOR TODAY'S CHILDREN

## Pooh shoes get straight A's for style and fit!

New Winnie-the-Pooh shoes for the smart set! All-leather uppers stay cleaner and newer-looking. Non-marking vinyl soles and heels last longer, too. With soft linings, cushioned insoles, and crush-resistant heel counters. Made to give growing feet sure fit and easy on-and-off. Brown or black ties, sizes 8½ to 4. Red, brown, or black buckle style, sizes 10 to 4. Only at Sears, Roebuck and Co. stores and through the catalog. Under $11.

The Shoe Place at

### Sears

He's lost in that uncharted territory where he's the fastest, strongest, roughest dude there ever was.

Maybe that's why he's wearing Little Levi's. Jeans and Koveralls™ made the same extra dependable way as grown up Levi's. They have rivets or bar tacking at every stress point. Double stitching (so they won't split at the seams). Heavy duty zippers. Even reinforced knees (in our Hardwear Jeans*).

So, Mom, when you're looking for truly durable clothes, in sizes 2-7, remember Little Levi's. They're built to "out-tough" the toughest kids.

# LITTLE LEVI'S. EVEN THE WILDEST CRITTERS CAN'T TAME THEM.

**Levi's**
YOUTHWEAR

QUALITY NEVER GOES OUT OF STYLE.

# Guess what inspired these new shoes.

**The Indy 500.**

It's a speed package crafted after the great high performance cars. A new shoe design inspired by the wild and mean machines.

Get into one where you buy fine footwear. Rev it up.

**The Purcell RaceAround.**

All the things that belong to the track now belong to this new shoe.

It's custom designed for movin' out. And movin' in.

All leather exterior. Air cooled. Cushion soles. Bumper-like toe guard. Tough rubber tread. Body by B. F. Goodrich.

On the rack. At your Purcell dealer's. Along with more than twenty other Purcell styles and colors to choose from.

**Get it on.**

*Jack Purcell, 1972*

"I can play better than you.
'Cause I practice every day.
I wear P.F Flyers. And
my dad is Hank Aaron".

When your dad is Hank Aaron, you get a lot of good tips on how to play a better game. Like wearing a shoe that helps you outplay the competition.

That's why Hank Aaron, right fielder for the Atlanta Braves, has young Hank wear P.F Flyers. Because they help young Hank to run faster, cut sharper and keep going longer.

It's the Posture Foundation® wedge inside each heel that does it, by helping feet to work the right way. The Posture Foundation is what the P.F in our name stands for. And only our shoes have it.

So take a hint from young Hank Aaron.

Get your dad to buy you P.F Flyers.

**P.F**

**P.F FLYERS.**
The only one with the wedge.

**B.F.Goodrich** ...in pursuit of excellence

*PF Flyers, 1971*

# Tapping their way to stardom

What every kid knows is that where it's at
is where it was. Like twirly skirts. And cowboy
shirts. And ingenue dresses. And plaids,
paisley and patchwork prints. All the great
looks of the past that are the great looks of
today.

1. Polyester and cotton turtleneck rib knit shirt. Assorted patterns. (Plum shown). S, M, L fits sizes 2
to 7. $2.99. Plum brushed cotton and polyester jeans. No ironing needed. 3 to 7. $3.49.
2. Cotton suede vest in navy, tan and wine. $6. Knickers in navy and wine. 7 to 14. $6.
3. Two-piece cotton corduroy suit. Contrasting cotton suede trim. Tan with brown or brown with tan.
14 to 20. $17.99.

4. Belted HotPants jumpsuit of cotton velour. Orange, berry or navy. Jr. Petites 3 to 11. $16.
5. Polyester and cotton patchwork print shirt. 3-button cuffs. Gold, brown or navy patchwork print.
No ironing needed. 8 to 20. $3.99. Polyester brushed denim flare jeans, 4 patch pockets. No ironing
needed. Navy, brown or plum. Slim 8 to 18, regular 8 to 20. $4.99. Husky 10 to 20. $5.49.

*Montgomery Ward, 1971*

# Wards clothes for today's kids.

But Wards has made a change. All those yesteryear-looking clothes are made in right now, easy to care for fabrics. When we give your kids the clothes they want we give you the clothes you want them to have. Open a Wards "Charg-All" account. It makes shopping simpler in our stores and catalog.

**MONTGOMERY WARD** Wards. The unexpected.

# The one and only
# Fresh Lemon Elbow Rub
## comes in this familiar yellow package.

When your grandmother was your age, rough, dry elbows were an unsightly problem for a pretty girl. They still are.

But what grandma may not have known was that the same beauty treatment she used to make her hair shine is good for elbows, too.

It's the fragrant fresh lemon itself. Refreshing. Effective. And full of good things that come from the earth, not a laboratory.

Try our Fresh Lemon Elbow Rub and you'll see what we mean. Just cut a Sunkist fresh lemon in half and soak each elbow for a few minutes while you're reading or watching TV. The natural lemon juices will help soften the rough, dry skin...make it easier to scrub away. Leaves your elbows looking smoother.

The one and only Fresh Lemon Elbow Rub. It's at your grocer's.

☙ **Sunkist.**

For colorful new lemon wall poster with lots more ideas about lemons for beauty, send 25¢ to Sunkist Growers, Inc., Dept. S9-73, 14130 Riverside Dr., Sherman Oaks, Calif. 91403. Sunkist is a trademark of Sunkist Growers, Inc. ©1973.

# Long & Silky.™ It silkens your hair without making it oily like some of those after-shampoo things can.

Some hair care things were made for everybody — and their mother.
And that's just why they're wrong for long hair. *Your* hair. *Your* look.
They can leave your hair looking just oily enough to spoil the whole effect.
But Long & Silky conditioning lotion was made just for you.
To give you the swings, not the strings. It helps split ends and tangles, all those things.
But somehow it all seems to rinse out clean.

Try it. You'll see.

# BRYLCREEM SAYS DON'T MEASURE YOUR SEX APPEAL BY THE LENGTH OF YOUR HAIR.

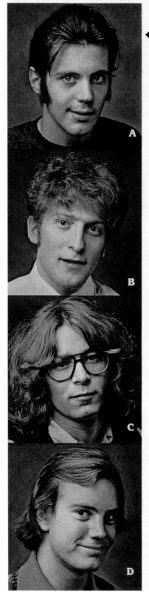

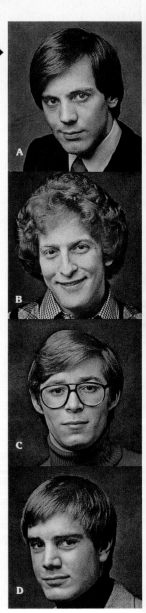

← **NOT SEXY**        **SEXY** →

**A.** Sideburns too long and too wide. End result: not too terrific. We said goodbye to sideburns and let his hair grow 1½ inches all over. Then gave it a layered cut.

Also recommended: frequent shampooing with Brylcreem Once A Day Shampoo to condition the hair while washing away excess oil, dirt and loose dandruff.

**B.** This guy was fighting natural curl with a cut that was too closely cropped on sides and back. We let it grow for two months and shaped it.

Because curly hair is porous and tends to dry out quickly, we used a dab of Brylcreem to condition while helping to keep the hair neat and manageable all day.

**C.** Too much hair, too little face. We took off 5 inches. Gave him a scissor cut, parted on the side to add more width and fullness to the top.

When hair goes through this change from very long to short, it needs about a week to lay right. Help it along with Brylcreem Power Hold, a specially formulated control hair spray that provides real holding power all day.

**D.** This guy's hair was all wrong for the shape of his face. Too long in back and too much of one length.

We cut off 2½ inches in front, 3 inches in back. We layered it on top for more body and gave him a geometric cut along the edges for the New Short look.

Brylcreem believes that sexy is as sexy does. And when your hair really does something for you, then you've got sex appeal.

## The Brylcreem group.

We've come a long way since "a little dab'll do ya."

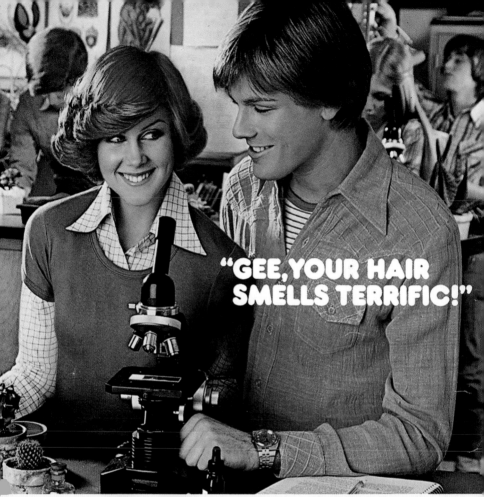

## "GEE, YOUR HAIR SMELLS TERRIFIC!"

"Gee, Your Hair Smells Terrific" is the shampoo made to leave hair smelling terrific. With a soft, young breezy-fresh fragrance. Like meadows of wildflowers in spring. But that's not all. "Gee" makes hair feel super-clean, too. Leaves it soft, silky and very shiny. Because isn't that why you wash your hair in the first place? "Gee, Your Hair Smells Terrific" Shampoo and same-fragrance Conditioner. Try them both and see: they're terrific!

## FRAGRANCE SHAMPOO & FRAGRANCE CONDITIONER.

Available in normal/dry and oily hair formulas.

Fabergé Presents

### COUNTRY★WESTERN COLORS

Natural earthtones for lips and nails
now going on in Fabergé country.

Go west, young girl. Follow the sun's warmest tones. Head for the Fabergé.

For Nails: Chestnut, Sunset, Fawn, Redwood, Pink Dawn, Soft Sienna, Sherry. / For Lips: Prairie Brown, Midnight Bronze, Dusty Coral, Desert Sand, Burnt Russet.

*Fabergé, 1974*

► *Breck, 1974*

# BRECK GIRL

Dianne Harris of Denver, Colorado.

Housewife, tennis player, skier,
ceramics hobbyist, graduate of
Colorado State University.

Dianne is a second generation Breck Girl.
Her mother first selected Breck, for beautiful hair.
And now her son, Courtney, follows the tradition,
at the age of seven.

*There's only one leading shampoo
that isn't mostly detergent:
Gold Formula Breck.*

# THE T-SHIRTERY INC.

**CUSTOM PRINTED SHIRTS, JERSEYS, AND KNITS**

The T-Shirtery Inc., 1976

► Coats & Clark, 1973

# Motorcycles are a thing with Karen and Carl. He does a great quiche lorraine. She's into Yoga. He makes their jewelry.

## She made these clothes.

Whatever Karen and Carl do, you can be sure they're expressing themselves. Together and singly. Take their clothes. It's Karen's very own form of self-expression, but they were created by her with their individual personalities in mind. Nice to know our threads, zippers and tapes had something to do with it. Look for them at notion counters and fine stores everywhere.

## COATS & CLARK

The leaders in sewing notions for over 160 years. Who could possibly know more about sewing?

# Our proving grounds.

Proving that the Forest Hills is adidas' lightest and most advanced tennis shoe required a unique series of scientific experiments: championship tennis matches. Matches which helped verify that its 8.7 ounce* weight made it easier to keep going...even after three gruelling hours.

Matches that aided in demonstrating the sophisticated adjustable sole ventilation system could keep inside temperatures 20% lower.

Matches that assisted in proving the specially developed Polaire sole to be five times more durable than ordinary soles.

The adidas Forest Hills. It took everything science knew about tennis and turned it to your advantage.

*Men's size 8½.

*The Forest Hills adidas' lightest tennis shoe*

# adidas® ✦®
## The science of sport.

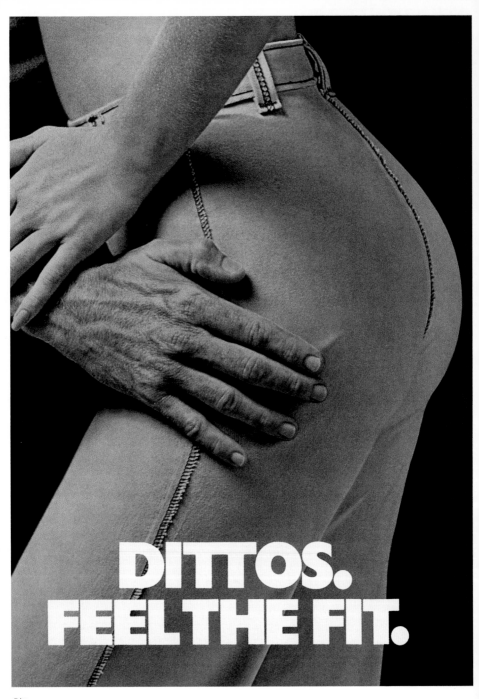

*Dittos, 1975*

# The world's best-fitting jeans.

Jeans never fit like this before. Because now every inch is accounted for!

Your exact waist size? You've got it. Exact leg length? It's yours. And imagine, the seat and thigh are proportioned so everything goes with everything else.

Put these jeans on and you'll know it's no put-on to say they're the best fitting jeans in the world.

Heavy denim and other rugged shape-holding jean fabrics that keep the fit perfect forever.

*chic* by

# h.i.s®

*Chic, 1978*

Jesus Jeans, 1976     ▶ Montgomery Ward, 1971

# You'll get a boot out of this.
## $5.88 a pair.

Where can you possibly find hook and eyelet lace-up boots, with side zippers, stretch shiny vinyl uppers, 1½ inch man-made heel, man-made soles, 16 inches high for $5.88 a pair?

At Wards. If you're ready for a boot, we're ready for you. In brown, black and white.

Open a Wards "Charg-All" account. It makes shopping simpler in our stores and catalogs.

MONTGOMERY
WARD

Wards. The unexpected.

**Modern Art**

Jantzen sets the new direction for swimwear in these *soft*, stylish knits. An action brief of DuPont ANTRON® nylon and LYCRA® spandex, a shirt of ANTRON. They're pure "Body Art"™ — from just one of the collections that makes Jantzen #1 in swimwear.

Jantzen

A source of pride
JANTZEN INC., PORTLAND, OREGON 97208

*Jantzen, 1976*

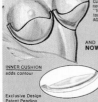

*Frederick's of Hollywood, 1975*

▶ *Frederick's of Hollywood, 1978*

# Macho. It's b-a-a-a-d.

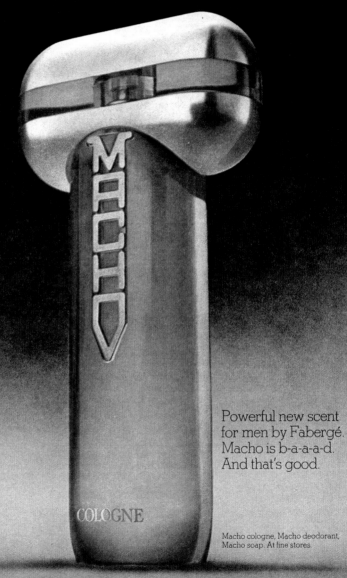

**MACHO**

COLOGNE

Powerful new scent
for men by Fabergé.
Macho is b-a-a-a-d.
And that's good.

Macho cologne, Macho deodorant,
Macho soap. At fine stores.

# Underfrance!

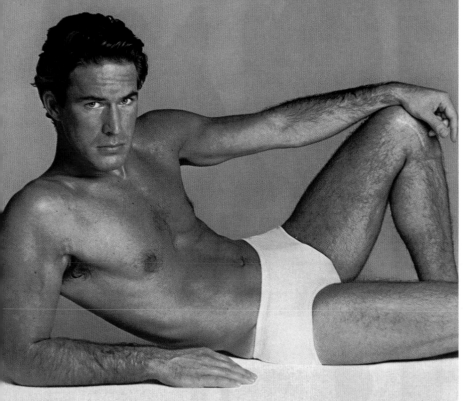

A few bare inches of smooth, supple, shape-showing maleness in soft Egyptian cotton. In colors that dare. In stores that care.

## Le French Brief by
## Eminence®
PARIS

Eminence International Inc., 12 West 18th Street, N.Y., N.Y. 10011.

# ENTERTAINERS.

# our name says it all.

Jump Suits, Ltd. began it all. And today, seven years later, is still a jump ahead.
Designing Jumpsuits in the newest, most natural fabrics.
Designing Jumpsuits which are young, hip, tight and sexy.
Designing jumpsuits which are made to fit.
When it comes to jumpsuits, we were first in fashion.... and we still are!

# JUMP SUITS®
## LTD.

A Division Of
**BRIGHT**
**RED**
**GROUP**

5526 E. Mockingbird / Dallas, Texas 75206
Telephone 214/826-8100
WRITE TO US FOR NEAREST DEALER AND CATALOG.

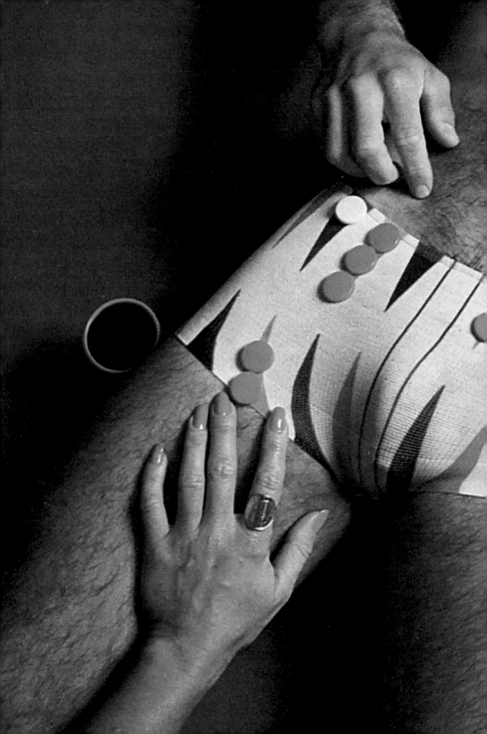

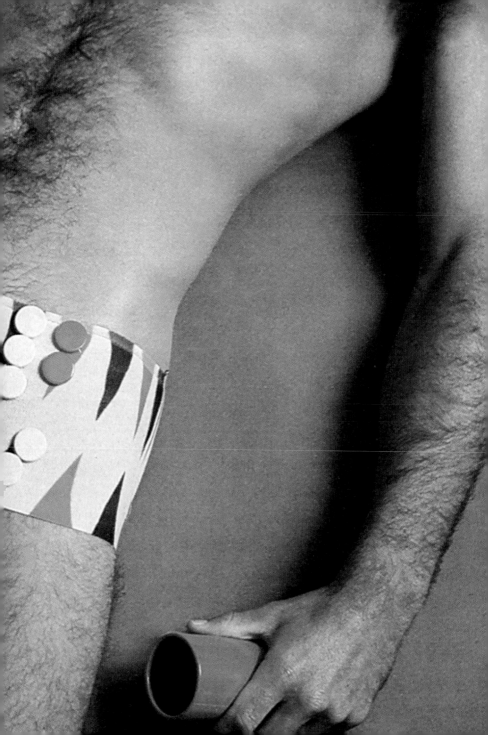

# OUR COLOR MAKES LIPS BEAUTIFU

# OUR MOISTURIZER THEM THAT W

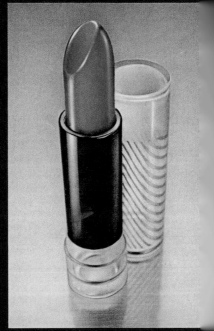

MAXI-MOIST L
WITH 83% MO
*only by* MAX FACT

Max Factor, 1977

# "Color me soft."

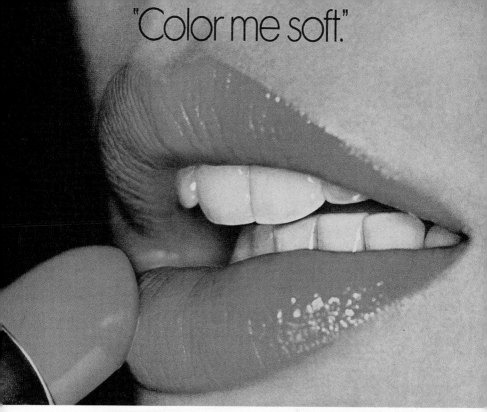

# Cover Girl creates
# 'LIP SOFTENERS'

**Don't just color your lips. Soften them, too.**
Cover Girl's special 'lip softening' formula makes taking care of your lips a super, soft job. Glides on nice and easy. Soft and creamy. Color is drenched with lip smoothing conditioners that moisturize and protect, too. Go ahead. Treat your lips to some super softness. (You've got 22 sumptuous shades to do it in!)

**COVER GIRL® 'LIP SOFTENERS'**™ LIPSTICKS THAT <u>SOFTEN</u> LIPS AS THEY COLOR

The Outspoken Chanel

N°19
CHANEL
PERFUME

Witty. Confident. Devastatingly feminine.
CHANEL N°19

*Halston Cosmetics, 1978*

▶ *Clinique, 1977*

# The Clinique Computer will see you now.

It will be a revelation.

In a quick 30-second consultation, you will learn your skin type, you will learn how to have better and better looking skin. Developed by a group of leading dermatologists, the fast, informative Clinique Computer Analysis is available at no charge at any Clinique Counter.

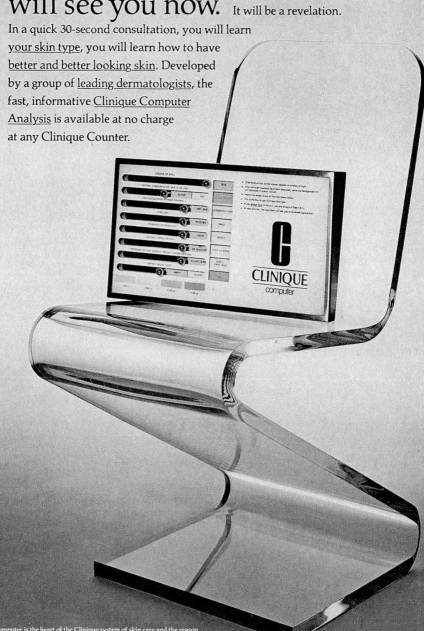

adidas 3-stripe warm ups, made in the exciting new Keyrolan fabric. Outside, Keyrolan shines like tinsel. Inside, it's as soft as feathers, with an Arnel nap, and is extra light and comfortable.

Horizontal fabric stretch provides a perfect fit for any figure — male or female. Durable and very easy to look after, they are ideal gifts for this festive season — for jingling or jogging!

The all-sports people

**KEYROLAN** ®

made for adidas by
BLUE RIDGE WINKLER
using ARNEL
TRIACETATE from
CELANESE

**adidas** ®

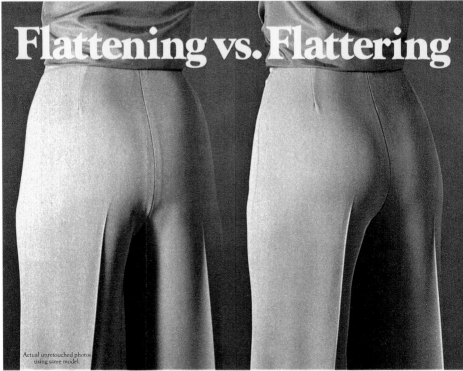

# Flattening vs. Flattering

Actual unretouched photos using same model.

## Sears Pretty Natural® Shaper.
## It's built like you are.

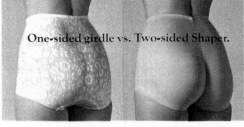

### One-sided girdle vs. Two-sided Shaper.

Sears Pretty Natural Shaper is constructed in two halves. So it conforms to your body. Firms you up. Rounds you out. And looks beautifully natural under clothes.

If flat is not your look, get into a Pretty Natural Shaper (or a Pretty Natural Shaper Plus for a little more control in the tummy). It'll make you look as womanly as you are. Only better.

THE FASHION PLACE

Sears

Available in most larger Sears retail stores and the catalog. © Sears, Roebuck and Co. 1978

SOFTMAGIC™
with reinforced panty/toe,
also in sheer-to-the-waist
and outsize. From $1.19*

PANTI-PANTYHOSE™
with cotton crotch, also in
control top and outsize.
From $1.49*

# Assorted Fruit

Pantyhose
from 99¢

BUDGETEER™
sheer-to-the-waist, also
with reinforced
panty/toe, 99¢*

GREAT SHAPE™
control top with sandal
foot, $1.99*. Also with
reinforced toe.
Outsize, $1.79
(not shown)

GREAT SHAPE™
sheer support, $2.99*

Whatever style fits your style,
you'll feel sheer, comfortable, confident.
And Assorted Fruit of the Loom
prices from 99¢* fit nicely in a budget
for a busy lifestyle, too.
Ask for them at
your favorite store.

FRUIT OF THE LOOM.
UNCONDITIONALLY GUARANTEED

*Manufacturer's suggested retail price.  Manufactured under license from Fruit of the Loom, Inc. • New York, NY

# Clairol® herbal essence shampoo.
## It does such beautiful things to your hair, and your head.

Come into the Garden of Earthly Delights.™
Where every bubble smells of mysterious green
herbs and freshly picked wildflowers. You'll leave
with the clean of a mountain stream and the
shine of the morning sun in your hair. And
beautiful thoughts of far, faraway places
in your head.

Experience Clairol® herbal essence
shampoo, a non-alkaline pH shampoo
with natural protein.

Your hair will get very excited.

© 1971·5 Clairol Inc.

clairol®
herbal
essence
shampoo
with
natural protein

*Clairol, 1975*

Jergens, 1975

# CAPTIVATING.

Major league Superstripes from **AJD** for Dads and Grads.

Available in the men's department at J.C. Penney.
Sized to fit men, women, and children.

**This is JCPenney**

# fashion knits from $6.96 to $15.96

Getting your fall wardrobe into shape doesn't have to put your budget out of shape. At K mart, you'll find all the great new sweater looks priced from $6.96 to $15.96. Wrap and zip front sweaters. Cowl neck and hooded styles. Big tops and tunic looks. The sweater styles to suit your life style. Warm 100% acrylic knits in an assortment of the newest fall colors. Look for them at over 1,100 K mart stores across the U.S.A.

**K mart**

The Saving Place

K mart Corporation  Troy, Michigan 48084

15.96

$15.96

$7.96

# The Olympic Pacesetters

Look at the
and your eyes will convince you tha
olympic athletes wear adida
other brands
The secret is that adidas make
shoe for the

## adidas ®

*Adidas, 1976*

Jockey International, Inc., Kenosha, Wisconsin 53140

# TAKE AWAY THEIR UNIFORMS AND WHO ARE THEY.

JOCKEY BRAND

Steve Garvey: Dual Purpose Underwear-Swimwear; Brad Park: Slim Guy, Nylon Boxer and T-Shirt; Lou Brock: Life® International Scandia Mesh A-Shirt/Brief;
Vic Hadfield: International Skants,® Metre Brief; Fred Dryer: Dual Purpose Sport Short; Craig Morton: International Skants,® Tropez Brief;
Terry Metcalf: Nylon A-Shirt/Brief; Ed Marinaro: Life® Bosun Shirt/Slim Guy Brief; Jim McMillian: Life® Denim Brief/A-Shirt.
Where to buy it? See page 189

*Jockey, 1976*

Steve Garvey/Los Angeles Dodgers

Brad Park/Boston Bruins

Lou Brock/St. Louis Cardinals

Vic Hadfield/Pittsburgh Penguins

Fred Dryer/Los Angeles Rams

Craig Morton/New York Giants

Terry Metcalf/St. Louis Cardinals

Ed Marinaro/Minnesota Vikings

Jim McMillian/Buffalo Braves

*Jockey, 1976*

The man's all legs and knows everything about feet. Listen:
"Boots have to look great—but they also have to be made for whatever you're going to be doing in them. That's why, when you say boots, you gotta say Dingo®."
Like O.J. Simpson, we mean what we say, and what we say is: Nobody Puts Leather Together Like Dingo.

dingo®

Nobody Puts Leather Together Like Dingo.

*Dingo, 1977*

Hanes, 1977

# Introducing Oleg Cassini's tennis whites. In smashing colors.

Oleg Cassini, avid tennis player.
Oleg Cassini, top fashion designer.
Who else could have created a smashing collection like the Oleg Cassini Tennis Club?

The *designer* in Cassini created the smashing colors and a sporting harmony in men's and women's outfits never before seen on the court.

But the *tennis player* in Cassini created the *fit*. It's pure tennis and ready for action. Every warm-up suit, sweater, jacket, dress, skirt, shirt and pair of shorts designed to *give* luxuriously. And cut to flatter too, like a Cassini original.

It doesn't look like ordinary tenniswear because it isn't. It's the Oleg Cassini Tennis Club.

And you're invited to join this season at a fine store near you.

Oleg Cassini by munsingwear

# The Oleg Cassini tennis club.

Oleg Cassini Division, Munsingwear, Minneapolis, Minnesota 55405

*Ralph Lauren, 1977* ◀

*Oleg Cassini, 1974*

# The big difference between us and them is the pocket. And the price.

The jeans with the fancy stitching on the back pocket are the world's best-selling jeans. They cost about $15.00. The jeans on the right are JCPenney Plain Pockets. They cost $10.00. Which would you rather have? A half-cent's worth of stitching on your pocket, or $5.00 in your pocket.

**Plain Pocket Jeans**
only at
**JCPenney**

The word "Levi's" is a registered trademark of Levi Strauss & Co., San Francisco, Calif. © 1977, Levi Strauss & Co.

**We asked our photographer to put <u>all</u> our denim in one picture.**

**He couldnt.** *Levis*

# The velour sportshirt that stays soft without getting flabby.

Too often, a soft velour shirt emerges from the wash with the collar mushy, the seams wobbly, the shoulders drooped.

This sort of flabby behavior is unacceptable to Van Heusen.

We make our Wimbledon velour sportshirt to stay the way it starts. Perfect.

We use the plushest velour, to give it body—it always hangs beautifully on your body. We knit it tighter than most, so it won't sag. We strengthen the seams, so they won't pucker. We construct the collar so it stays fresh.

When you buy a Wimbledon velour

sportshirt in any one of our elegant styles, patterns, or colors, it always looks the best on your shape. Because it keeps its own. *Wimbledon®* by

## VAN HEUSEN

**Next to ours, a good sportshirt isn't good enough.**

THE VAN HEUSEN COMPANY
A DIVISION OF THE PHILLIPS-VAN HEUSEN CORP

# Booting Now:
## The Classics, Winter '78 Style. At Kinney.

Thoroughbreds. Bootmaker crafted to keep busy feet feeling free through the day and into the night.

A mere hint of Kinney's boot bounty for the new season's casual, sporty and dress-up turnouts. From $24.99 to $42.99.

### Kinney®
The Great American Shoe Store

# bareback action!

High gear!
Polished woods
on layered bottoms
are generating
big fashion mileage.
Leather bareback, 21.99;
the smoothie, 18.99.

18.99 & 21.99

east of the Rockies **BAKERS • LEEDS** on the West Coast
QUALICRAFT® SHOE STORES

OO LA LA!

SASSON
jeans, inc.

*He can always spot the girl in Blue Jeans**

BLUE JEANS® cologne of course.

'OGRAPHED AT "NEW YORK, NEW YORK DISCOTHEQUE".          * BLUE JEANS IS A REGISTERED TRADEMARK FOR COLOGNE AND DUSTING POWDER.

# Jōvan has created a new generation of fragrances.

## So different, they don't just say who you are.
## They say what you are.

One is for him.
Man by Jōvan. The most masculine
aftershave/cologne ever.
A potent blend of leather,
tabac, and peppery spices.
With a surprising twist.

The other is for her.
Woman by Jōvan.
The ultimate fragrance.
A cologne concentrate.
Totally feminine. Intensely
floral. And softly seductive.

Man by Jōvan.                Woman by Jōvan.

And, just as it is in real life, Man and Woman come in different forms, shapes, and sizes. They are available at leading department and drug stores.
© 1977 Jōvan Inc., 875 N. Michigan Ave., Chicago, Illinois.

# THE ROOT OF ALL EVIL?

The Ginseng root has been blamed for centuries for the evils of the flesh.

While skeptical of its legendary aphrodisiac powers, English Leather has created a new men's cologne around this herbal root.

The result, a strangely gratifying effect on you and those around you. More than just a scent,

It's a mood that envelops.

Mysterious how something one person puts on himself can make two people lose their heads.

$5 at fine toiletry counters everywhere.

## GINSENG COLOGNE BY ENGLISH LEATHER®
The scent of the centuries.

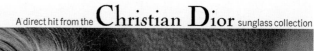

A direct hit from the **Christian Dior** sunglass collection

CHRIS VON WANGENHEIM

# Explosive is Your Dior.

# My men wear Interwoven socks and English Leather or...
# They wear nothing at all.

Depending on the time, the people, and the mood, a man can be dressed quite properly even when he's virtually undressed.

For example, a splash of English Leather for sex appeal and a pair of Interwoven socks for "socks" appeal can create the perfect ensemble for a night when he's not out on the town.

So give your man Interwoven Socks and English Leather Cologne this Christmas. After all, how else can you get a complete outfit for under $15.00?

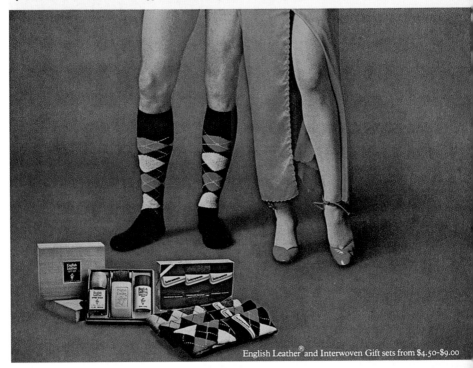

English Leather® and Interwoven Gift sets from $4.50-$9.00

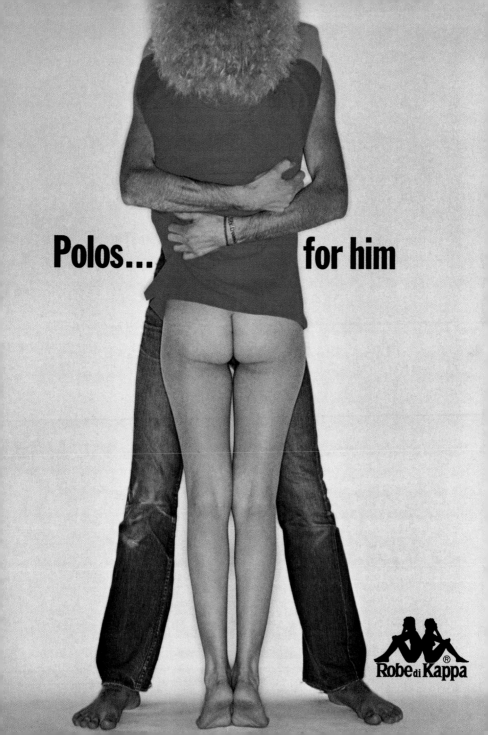

# Return to Paradise

with the underwear more comfortable than nothing at all! Adam Briefs' exciting new "Jean Look" print gives you the feel and fit of your favorite pair of jeans.   The next time you change underwear, experience Paradise with the casual comfort of Adam's exciting "Jean Look" briefs.

## Adam Briefs™
P.O. Box 4090
Beverly Hills, California 90213

*Adam Briefs, 1976*

Too skinny to have fun...
# SHAPE A NEW YOU

A chance to really be me. Imagine. To be noticed. To compete where I never thought I could. To really feel good about myself. Thank you Wate-On. You changed my life. I was really skinny because I just didn't eat right. It was really a drag. Wate-On's extra calories helped me fill-out . . . shape my whole body. Wate-On has vitamins, iron and minerals plus nutrients known for strength and energy. Wate-On works. Shape a new you. Ask your druggist for Wate-On . . . Super and Regular strength . . . in liquid, tablets and new energizer bars. Send for your FREE Guide to Successful Weight Gaining. Write: Wate-On® ,Dept. WO-000, 600 Hunter Drive, Oak Brook, Illinois 60521.

YES! Please send my FREE Guide to Successful Weight Gaining today.

NAME

ADDRESS

CITY                     STATE                ZIP
Wate-On® Dept. WO-41 , 600 Hunter Drive, Oak Brook, IL 60521

**Wate-On®**

*Wate-On, 1978*  ▶▶ *Revlon, 1978*

The frost that's a lipstick.
The frost that's a lip conditioner.
The frost that's a lipgloss.

Revlon creates Frost Formula 2.

The only lipfrost and lipgloss in one.
Colors. Conditions. Shines.

Frost Formula 2.
Now. From the Revlon Research Group.

# Resillience challenges the frail nail.

Give your nails a fighting chance. With new Resillience. The incredibly long-wearing, flexible nail enamel that stands up to chips, to cracks and splits. Coty fortifies Resillience with a unique Polyester Resin that has never before been used in a nail enamel. Blazes it with high glossers. And dazzles it with 14 high fashion colors, plus clear "Sparkling Glass." Then puts it in a very sensible spill-proof bottle. Wear new Resillience. And be a knock-out.

# New Resillience by Coty

© Coty, N.Y.

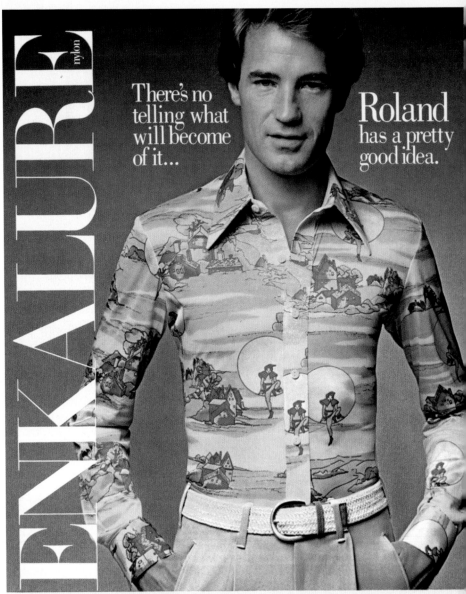

**There's no telling what will become of it...**

**Roland has a pretty good idea.**

You'll look current and feel comfortable when you put on this scenic shirt by Roland. The silky feel of the fabric, the with-it look of the print make the perfect top for the kind of leisure pants you live in. This contemporary shirt's made of Enkalure® nylon, today's kind of yarn for your kind of lifestyle. And perfect fit's a fact. This body shirt comes in six (count 'em six!) body-hugging sizes: small, small/medium, medium, medium/large, large and extra-large.

Available at fine men's wear stores everywhere.

Or contact Roland, Division of RK Industries, Inc., 936 Maple Ave., Los Angeles, Cal. 90015, for the store nearest you.

**ENKA**

ENKALURE IS A REG T M OF AMERICAN ENKA CO. ENKA N.C. A PART OF AkZona INC. FOR ITS MULTILOBAL NYLON YARN LICENSED FOR USE IN APPROVED FABRICS

# It must be harder to make a pair of Sansabelt® slacks than we thought.

It was 20 years ago when we first sewed a wide band of triple-stretch webbing into the waistband of a pair of our slacks. And the Sansabelt concept was born.

For us, it was simple. But then, we had already been making terrific men's slacks for over 40 years.

For the world in general, it was a revolution. Never before did a pair of slacks have so much going for it. The fit. The styles. The fabrics—like 100% Trevira® polyester. And, of course, the unique patented Sansabelt concept.

It all helped Sansabelt become the largest-selling dress slack model in the country. By a comfortable margin.

After 20 years, no one has come close to duplicating our simple idea.

But then, maybe it's harder to do than we thought.

**SANSABELT®**

The Sansabelt Suit

## JAYMAR
### Where slacks are only the beginning.

**KAREN BLACK**

## Some women are more alive than others.

Part of it has to do with the woman.
The other part has to do with Alive.
Alive is the support pantyhose from
Hanes. For you and every woman who works
hard, plays hard and loves being alive.
So beautiful, Karen Black wears it.
Even under the lights.

**Alive® Support Pantyhose by Hanes.**
Available in a variety of styles and colors at finer department and apparel stores.

# The slacks for the fashion conscious man. From the comfort conscious company.

It's hard enough to find a good looking pair of slacks. It's even harder to find a good looking pair of slacks that are comfortable.

Introducing Jay-Bonair.® The best looking collection of slacks you've ever seen. And the most comfortable you've ever put on.

The Jay-Bonair Collection from Jaymar features the European look and the dress jean look. In a huge selection of colors, patterns and fabrics like Burlana.* The fabric with a rich, natural touch. Made possible by two special kinds of Dacron** polyester combined with wool.

As for the comfort, they're tailored by Jaymar. And that's all that really has to be said.

## JAYMAR
### Where slacks are only the beginning.

**Encron Strialine.
The first slub filament polyester.
It puts a little texture in your line,
for a change.**

Latitudes™
by Phoenix.

The secret of looking like an individual in leisurewear is classic styling with individual-looking fabric. This leisuresuit by Phoenix sports fabric with an interesting slubby look. It's knit of Encron® Strialine,® the fiber that gives fabric the look of total texture. Still, Encron Strialine is polyester. And easy to care for.

Available at fine department and specialty stores everywhere. Or contact Phoenix Clothes, a Div. of Genesco, 1290 Avenue of the Americas, New York, N.Y. 10019, for the store nearest you.

**ENKA**

*Enka, 1976*

**Classic White Knits**—Casually sophisticated. That sums up this Lee trend-setter featuring a shirt jacket (about $30) with epaulets and enamel-like buttons and matching slacks (about $20). Both are defined twill double-knits of non-glitter 100% Dacron® polyester. The sports shirt (about $17) tops off another great "Tops & Bottoms" idea from The Lee Company, 640 Fifth Ave., N.Y., N.Y. 10019. **Lee**™ A company of V͡F corporation

*Lee, 1975*

## Johnny Miller Menswear.
## Sears smart new approach to the classics.

This Fall, the look in menswear is clearly classic. You'll see it in superbly cut blazers of pure wool, in soft cotton velour pullovers, in rich tartan slacks.

It's a great look. And Sears makes it look smarter than ever with exceptional tailoring, fresh details, and clear, clean colors.

Another smart thing: Because it's at Sears, this fine collection comes with very sensible prices.

See Johnny Miller Menswear only in selected larger Sears stores. Blazers, $85. Slacks, $32. Shirts, $15-$17. Prices higher in Alaska.

©Sears, Roebuck and Co. 1976

SHIRT, $29.00; SLACKS, $48.50; KNIT TURTLENECK, $15.00; ROBE, $55.00; MOTOR ROBE, $30.00; DOUBLEKNIT SWEATER, $60.00; MUFFLER, $8.50; CAP, $8.00.

Pendleton, USA. It's a world of better sportswear in the good taste
and comfort of 100% virgin wool. Created with the care for quality
and value that's been a part of our world for four generations.
This Christmas, heighten the joy of giving and receiving. In Pendleton,
USA. Happy Holidays. For further information write Dept. N,
Pendleton Woolen Mills, Portland, Oregon 97201.

WARRANTED TO BE A
"PENDLETON"
TRADE MARK REG US PAT OFF
PENDLETON WOOLEN MILLS
PORTLAND, OREGON
100% VIRGIN WOOL

ALL PURE WOOL

# Christmas in
# Pendleton USA.

The City Cowboy Collection

Fashion excitement! The Look for Fall. Nobody brings the West to the city better than that designer of finely-crafted leather footwear, Giorgio Brutini. What are you waiting for, pardner?

**GIORGIO BRUTINI**
paris    madrid    são paulo

A Division of **harbor** IMPORTS

350 Fifth Avenue, N.Y.C. (212) 695-3880

At the stores listed.

*Giorgio Brutini, 1979*

▶ *Washington Manufacturing Company, 1976*

# Go West with the folks who know the trail.

Everybody's riding shotgun today, Cheyenne to Chicago. And for pure-bred western looks, nobody knows the West better than DEE CEE. We dress the cowboy on the ranch or on the town. We know the territory...from way back.

## Washington Manufacturing Company
Division of Washington Industries **WI** Nashville, Tennessee

Hard drivin' and fast livin' can
leave a man plumb wore out. But his
Levi's for Feet boots will
keep goin' strong.

# Levi's for feet

Available in fine stores everywhere

**Levi's**
®

QUALITY NEVER GOES OUT OF STYLE.

Geoffrey Beene

# Wrangler

**Wrangler thinks Americans should get what they pay for.**

**That's your right and our responsibility.**

**Tomorrow's looks today in Jackets and Jeans.**

Wrangler Menswear
330 Fifth Avenue
New York 10001
© 1977 by Blue Bell, Inc.

# INTRODUCING THE
# World's first cologne exclusively for gay men.

*Reo, 1978*

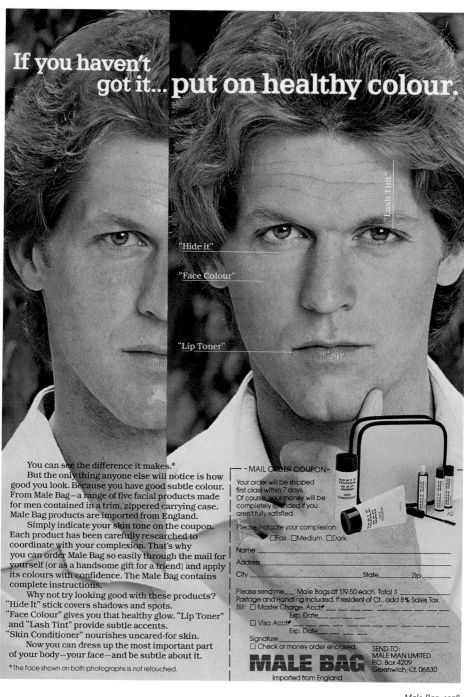

# If you haven't got it... put on healthy colour.

"Lash Tint"

"Hide it"

"Face Colour"

"Lip Toner"

You can see the difference it makes.*
But the only thing anyone else will notice is how good you look. Because you have good subtle colour. From Male Bag—a range of five facial products made for men contained in a trim, zippered carrying case. Male Bag products are imported from England.

Simply indicate your skin tone on the coupon. Each product has been carefully researched to coordinate with your complexion. That's why you can order Male Bag so easily through the mail for yourself (or as a handsome gift for a friend) and apply its colours with confidence. The Male Bag contains complete instructions.

Why not try looking good with these products? "Hide It" stick covers shadows and spots. "Face Colour" gives you that healthy glow. "Lip Toner" and "Lash Tint" provide subtle accents. "Skin Conditioner" nourishes uncared-for skin.

Now you can dress up the most important part of your body—your face—and be subtle about it.

*The face shown on both photographs is not retouched.

*Male Bag, 1978*

THE
JORDACHE
LOOK

JORDACHE®
Designer Jeans by R. Jordache

Showroom: 110 E 9 th St. L.A. CA 90079 213 624 1992

Available in San Francisco at:
Emporium, Gloding's, I. Magnin, J. Magnin,
Liberty House, Macy's, Roos Atkins.

Available in Los Angeles at:
Aprés Apropos Look, The Broadway, Bullock's,
Double-up Stores, Fred Segal Jeans, I. Magnin,
Inspiration, J. Magnin, J. W. Robinson,
Nobody, Peaches, Pigeon, The Corral,
Fix Rack Inc., The Corral,
Wild West Stores, Windsor Fashion.

*Jordache, 1979*

▶ *Famolare, 1979*

'GET THERE'

'GET THERE'

'ELEGET'

'GET THERE'

'HI UP'

# Raves for Waves

UNIQUE WAVE-SOLE CREATIONS FOR MEN, WOMEN
AND CHILDREN DESIGNED BY JOE FAMOLARE

## FAMOLARE®
PUTS AMERICA ON ITS FEET ™
4 East 54th St., New York, N.Y. 10022

# the pierre cardin visual experience.

A fantastic new collection of sunglasses and frames for men of fashion.

## pierre cardin

Fur by Oliver Gintel.

SECURITY GUARD

# The Maidenform woman.
# You never know where she'll turn up.

Now she's turned up in
something luxurious enough
to bank on. Sweet Nothings
underwire. Excitingly romantic
with a delicate touch of lace.
Also available in soft cup,
demi-bra or light fiberfill. All
front-close in lots of high interest
colors. Underwire bra from $9.
All with matching Bikini.

## Sweet Nothings® Underwire
## by Maidenform®

Made with **Antron** Du Pont registered trademark. Lace: nylon. Tricot: "Antron III"
nylon. Back "Antron" nylon. "Lycra" spandex. Exclusive of decoration.
Prices are suggested retail. Prices higher in Canada.

*Pierre Cardin, 1976* ◀

*Maidenform, 1979*

After five, it's Climax and Nyesta®...a hint of yes.

For that intimate evening
at Orsini's.
You'll look so good.
You'll feel so good.
"Of course, it's Nyesta®."
It's a way of life.

Dresses by **Climax**, division of David Howard of California, and other fine fashions of **Nyesta®** fabric are featured at all **Paraphernalia stores** in: Atlanta, Ga., Chattanooga, Tenn., Columbia, Md., Exton, Pa., Garden City, N.Y., Lawrenceville, N.J., Langhorne, Pa., Paramus, N.J., San Francisco, Calif., West Farms, Conn., Worcester, Mass., and Chestnut Street, Philadelphia, Pa.

*Climax, 1976*

▶ *Funky, 1976*

# FUNKY.

# When you want to be seen in all the best places.

Funky's Great Show-off Dress, Style 328, a head-turning number in softly daring Dupont Antron® nylon Nyesta® by Roselon, $70. In White, Shrimp and 20 other irresistible colors. Sizes 3 to 15. So call Funky toll-free 800-421-2062* and show off your shape, baby.

*Except Alaska and Hawaii. In California call: 213-749-1481.
Executive Offices: 1301 South Hope Street, Los Angeles, Ca. 90015.

**Funky** ® **nyesta** 100% DuPont nylon

The Mistress Collection.

OPIUM par Yves Saint Laurent.
Jamais parfum n'a provoqué une telle émotion.

*Parfums*
YVESSAINTLAURENT

Yves Saint Laurent, 1979

▶ *Gucci, 1979*

There can never be too much elegance in your life.

**CHAZ**

The fragrance that's almost as interesting as the men who wear it.

CHAZ for men by Revlon. Cologne, After Shave, Soap and Talc.

It was made to be worn.

The Ralph Lauren Western Collection.

**Fashion Now 2**
Eds. Terry Jones & Susie
Rushton / Flexi-cover, 640 pp. /
€ 29.99 / $ 39.99 / £ 24.99 /
¥ 5.900

**Fashion from the 18th to the
20th Century** The Kyoto
Costume Institute / Flexi-cover,
192 pp. / € 6.99 / $ 9.99 /
£ 5.99 / ¥ 1.500

**60s Fashion. Vintage
Fashion and Beauty Ads**
Ed. Jim Heimann / Flexi-cover,
192 pp. / € 6.99 / $ 9.99 /
£ 5.99 / ¥ 1.500

## "These books are beautiful objects, well-designed and lucid." —*Le Monde*, Paris, on the ICONS series

## " Buy them all and add some pleasure to your life."